THE F.E.W. PRESENTS

LADIES OF THE NIGHT

OWN YOUR POWER IN MUSIC ENTERTAINMENT AND BUSINESS

Edited by:
David Goode, Keyoka Kinzy and The F.E.W

Book Formatting: Write on Promotions

Cover by:
Write on Promotions

ISBN: 979-8-218-48815-4

Registered with the Library of Congress.

Printed and manufactured in the United States of
America.

Table of Contents

Table of contents

FORWARD:
DJ Thump

When it comes to storytelling through music, DJ Kelly J is a master at it. Her high energy and fun flava makes any event a memorable journey. She studied and mastered her craft and became a dominating force in the industry. Her passion for the culture drove her to teach the art of DJ'ing at UNLV, giving each of her students the proper tools to evolve.

NotaboiDJ also controls her audience with her innovative mixes and infectious energy. She has cultivated a loyal following of music lovers who can't get enough of her unique sound. Her Chicago style and addition of West Coast seasoning drastically separates her from other DJs. It's clear these ladies are not female DJs...They are DJs who happen to be women.

Angie T is a master of her craft. Her smooth vocals and engaging stage presence adds an extra layer of excitement to every performance, capturing the hearts and souls of audiences wherever she goes. With an undeniable passion for music and a commitment to pushing the boundaries of creativity, Angie T is sure to leave a lasting impression on anyone lucky enough to experience her magic firsthand.

With their years of radio and club experience, together they are a force to be reckoned with.

So sit back, relax, and get ready to be taken on a journey like no other with DJ Kelly J, NotaboiDJ, and Angie T. Trust me, you won't be disappointed.

Dr. Ni'Cola Mitchell

To my Goddaughter, DJ Kelly J, and her beautiful friends, Angie T and Notaboi DJ—watching you ladies grow in your crafts has been an absolute pleasure and a true testament to what tenacity looks like. You each embody the fierce determination, unyielding passion, and relentless drive that it takes to succeed in an industry that can be as tough as it is thrilling.

"Bars & Beats: Ladies of The Night" is a gripping, no-holds-barred dive into the wild, exhilarating, and sometimes scandalous world of the entertainment industry. Written by three powerhouse women—Kelly J, Angie T, and NAB—this book is your ultimate streetwise guide to making it big in music, radio, and event hosting.

Kelly J, my Goddaughter, sets the tone with her raw and unfiltered account of the hustle behind the scenes. She's broken barriers, smashed through obstacles, and emerged as a force to be reckoned with. Her journey is a testament to grit, perseverance, and the power of believing in your magic.

Angie T, The Voice, steps up with her fierce confidence, delivering sharp, witty insights that reveal the secrets to commanding the stage and captivating audiences. Her story is one of bold chances, personal growth, and embracing life on her terms. Angie's journey inspires all of us to live authentically and shine brightly, no matter the odds.

NAB rounds out this dynamic trio, sharing her rise from the corporate grind to becoming a top DJ and radio personality. Her tale is filled with highs, lows, and nonstop beats, highlighting the transformative power of passion and persistence. NAB's story reminds us of the importance of mentorship, friendship, and chasing dreams with unrelenting determination.

Throughout "Bars & Beats: Ladies of The Night," you'll find street-smart tips, jaw-dropping stories, and hardcore motivation. This book is more than a guide—it's a masterclass in resilience, spirituality, self-care, and financial savvy, all delivered with the kind of wisdom that only comes from women who have lived it.

To my ladies—Kelly J, Angie T, and NAB—your journeys inspire me and so many others. May this book empower all who read it to push beyond their limits and live out their wildest dreams. Keep shining, keep hustling, and keep making magic. The world needs your light.

PREFACE:
(How it started)

All of the signs pointed to us writing a book; we literally have the spiritual messages to prove it. There isn't a manual on how to navigate the entertainment industry, nor have we ever had a space to be transparent about the many experiences we've encountered thus far. We wanted to be able to help and motivate others as well as offer guidance to those wanting to get into the business. Consider this book the cheat code! Just to be clear, some names, companies and places have been modified to protect our asses!

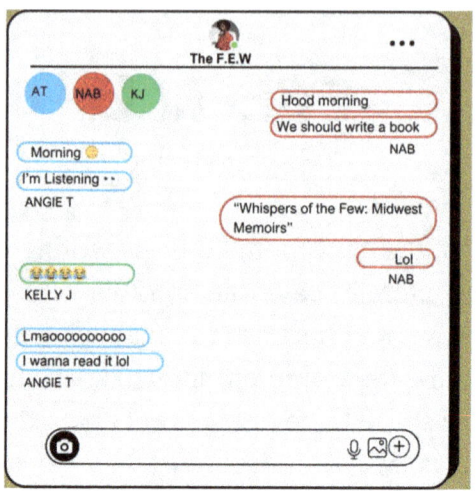

NAB: *It was a random thought in my head like most of my ideas, where I just felt that we should collectively put all of our mistakes, successes, and dramas in a book!*

Kelly J: *There's a new idea in the group chat every other week it seems, but this time I was on board. The idea of a book crossed my mind a number of times already, and doing one with Ang and NAB was sure to be a great one. So, half awake, I'm like, "uhm, okay!"*

Angie T: *Tbh we have 1,001 ideas a week so even though this wasn't a bad or unobtainable idea. I still wasn't sure if we were for real for real. Writing a book* *was something I always wanted to do. As a Host/Emcee, I feel like a book is a trophy piece, so I knew if we all were in alignment that it would be huge! I decided to wait to see if it came back around for us then I'd know we should move forward.*

- <u>Dec. 28, 2023</u>
(Screenshot from Angie T)

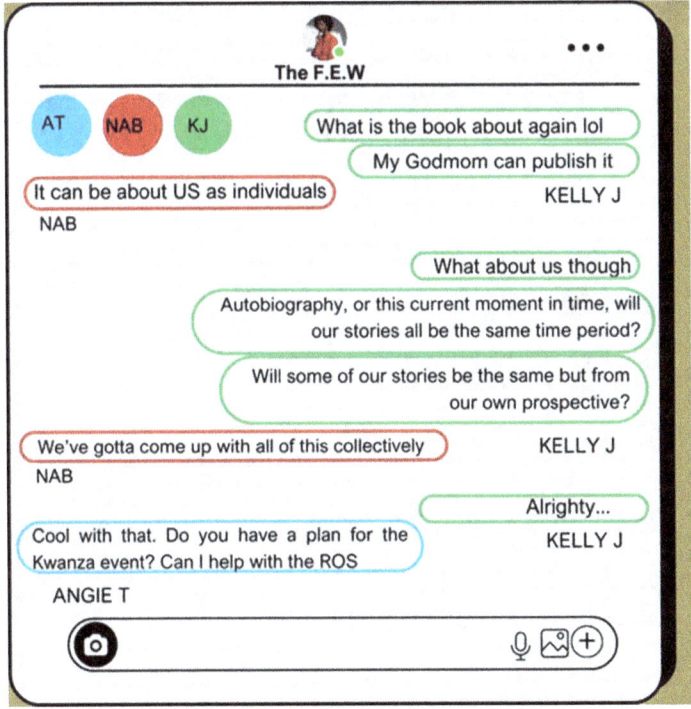

NAB:*(Did yall notice how Angie's ass didn't even respond?)*

Angie T: *To my defense I felt like I agreed with the group and didn't have anything new to suggest. I acknowledged the conversation and moved on to more immediate tasks. Because I knew we would discuss it later when we saw each other, still not 1,000% sure if we were going to do this but remained open to the progress we were all willing to make.*

- April 15, 2024, One day Kelly J was over NAB's house to bring her daughter her b-day gift and they were revisiting the conversation about doing a book, but within moments Angie T texted the group chat after her flight landed:

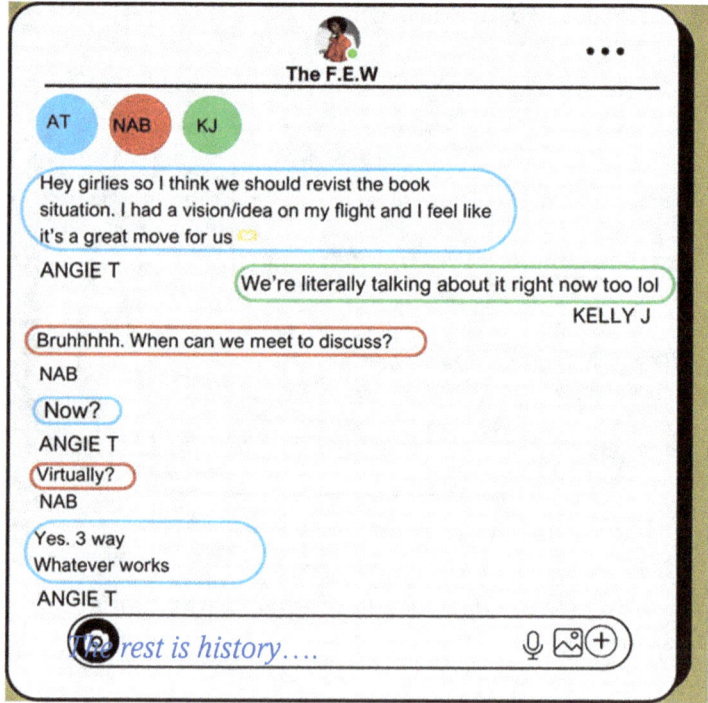

INTRO:
Let's Get It Started

NAB:

I'm NotaboiDJ, aka Fire (the F in The F.E.W.), aka NAB. Contrary to popular belief I'm an air sign, a vivacious Gemini to be precise but I exude a hell of a lot of fire energy. Not to mention I quite often parade around with red hair like a Phoenix rising from the ashes. I'm the one that's going to speak up when no one else will. According to me, I know when to hold & when to fold but at the end of the day I need everyone to know that I don't have goofy written on my forehead. If I have to stand up for the underdogs I'm more than qualified to do so and will happily volunteer as tribute. I feel like it's my duty to speak up. Before it was trendy, I always said what I said…with my chest! Spontaneous combustion will surely be the death of me if I don't say what needs, better yet must be said. (Some may call me dramatic, but I call it passionate). I have no qualms about running into battle head first with my blood red colored lace front or faux locs, without any army or a peanut gallery to back me up. What can I say? I actually like the sport (fighting) I mean boxing! Bail money is always on deck! Plus, I stay prayed up!

The Gemini in me is either going to meditate, over-think, & rationalize orrrrrrrr take it too far, risk everything, & blame the alleged victim for making me act out of character. IJS I'm pretty good at self-control so if YOU make me act a fool then it most certainly is YOUR fault. After all, maybe I was sent from your guardian angels to teach you a lesson? Right? (You can thank me later) The funny thing about it is people never know what side of me they'll get & quite frankly... I don't know either.

With all of that being said, I can guarantee that I have stellar work ethics, I'm fluid enough to where I can walk in any room and act accordingly, and I can be as professional as I need to be. Reliable and responsible are some pretty adjectives that we can use to add to my colorful character. At any rate, you can call me Notaboi or NAB! Nice to meet cha! That's my name...I paid for it so that's what you can call me or don't call me at all! I'm a DJ/On Air Personality who randomly signed up for DJ classes at a Guitar Center some odd years ago while taking my daughter there to purchase stuff for her Ukulele. I literally walked in and was like oh they have DJ classes and I just got my income taxes which means I should do something responsible and productive with my new riches right? Sign me up! That's me...the type of person that sometimes just does stuff. And guess what? Most times it pays off! People don't always understand my moves but it never stops me from making them. Ultimately, this small investment and random ass decision changed my life forever.

Let's take it back. Growing up playing the piano and singing I never could have imagined that I would end up in an industry which places me at the epicenter of music. Sometimes I think my life is a dream and I'm scared that I might wake up one day back inside of corporate America working in a cube farm. As a child, my mother sang and toured often so I was always going to her rehearsals, auditions, & shows. There were countless moments where my house was transformed into practices and meetups which sometimes included me practicing and helping her and her bandmates with harmonizing, finding the right keys, learning octaves, etc.

Most certainly, this upbringing contributed to me having an ear for music. When I wasn't with her, I was with my aunts that were very heavily involved in church. I vividly remember falling asleep many days in the church pews while they sang their hearts out to sweet baby Jesus. I also remember puking all over the pews one night after consuming an ungodly amount of ranch salad dressing (I still hate that shit - the dressing I mean…to this day). Spending weekends with them involved more singing, and more rehearsals. Sometimes my cousin would come over and we would have our own private concerts. She would be Whitney while I was Mariah or she was Monica and I was Brandy.

My older brother is a musical genius. He self-taught himself how to play a plethora of instruments. Sometimes he would play his clarinet outside and butterflies would come sit on him as if he was "Peter the Piper in the flesh. Prince was his #1 inspiration which obviously made me a fan…I mean who doesn't like Prince? (If it's you then keep that shit to yourself). Being the genius that he is, my brother filled my soul with eclectic artists like Alanis Morrisette, Duran Duran, Terrance Trent D'Arby and so forth.

We spent hours singing and performing in our homemade basement band without a spectator in sight. He even bought me a violin! Holidays were full of talent shows in my family. It was mandatory for all of the kids to put on some type of musical performance in front of everyone. They always cheered us on but I'm sure the dranks in their cups wasn't holy water and it made them believe that we sounded phenomenal. One Christmas I performed "Thuggish Ruggish Bone" with my cousins bruhhhhhh…never again.

Once I was old enough to put my foot down, I did. However, that didn't stop my mother from signing me up for modeling and singing contests. I performed all the way up into my early adult years which left me with an awful case of stage fright. I'm sure eventually the footage from those performances will surface and I'll be painstakingly embarrassed. To this day, I do not like getting on the microphone. I've been getting better but I'd much rather speak with my hands, through the music and if need be, with a right hook! I mean I just love music so much that I can't stand when other people talk over songs either. Music has always been my therapy. When life gets too heavy for me to bear I still run to my keyboard and melt into the melodies that I produce until I'm ready to face the world again.

Some sounds are so sweet to me that I can taste them…for example any Marvin Gaye song. His music soothes my spirit like no other. While other songs stink so good that I can smell them…like the early weezy f baby days. Have you ever heard a beat that makes you squint your eyes, scrunch up your nose, turn down your lips, & rock your head back & forth? If not... I hate that for you. Did I mention that I'm passionate? In an unsuccessful attempt to go into labor, my mother told me how she would do Michael Jackson's "Thriller" dance repeatedly. Well let's just say I definitely came out a dancing machine (pun intended). I will DJ & dance all over the place with any and everybody, teaching line dances to the whole world (just don't ask me to grab the mic). Ok! I mean even if somebody lost their keys, is parked in a tow zone, or it's your great grandmother's 365th birthday. DON'T ASK ME. Better yet, here's the mic...you tell'em!

I literally slid in Kelly's dms and told her that I was a new DJ and wanted her to mentor me. Although she stated that she was unable to be my mentor, she allowed me to shadow her at pretty much all of her events. I was like, "Say less!" Every chance I could get, I popped up everywhere she Dj'd. Gig after gig after gig after gig, I would follow her around and absorb the way she rocked crowds. Paying extra close attention to how she managed song requests/demands, missed meals, bladder control, ego driven men, late hours, lifting heavy ass equipment, and oh so much more, I decided to join the madness.

The ability to shift the energy of a room by the flick of a wrist and the right song selection captivated my entire being. I owe the phenomenal DJ Kelly J half of my billions as soon as the check clears. She to this day has been the most instrumental in my success and I am forever in her debt. Shortly after we met, I began working at KCEP 88.1FM a Las Vegas radio station that she coincidentally worked at as well. Divine timing like a mf.

This is also where I met the sensational Angie T. She was an on-air personality at the same radio station. Initially, I didn't really care for some of her choice of words towards me so I figured we would just be co-workers butttttttttt I was wrong. First impressions aren't always the best impression after all. As time went on, us three worked so close together and curated a multitude of events collectively that we figured it only made sense for us to form a group. Due to the fact that we were all into astrological and spiritual practices, we came up with the name, "The F.E.W." (Fire, Earth, and Wind).

KELLY J:

I'm Kelly J aka Earth out of the F.E.W. I'm a Taurus in EVERY way, but people can never guess my sign off the bat. Everyone senses the earth in me though. When I finally say, my zodiac sign, some variation of "oh yeaaaaah!" follows. Because my upbringing has been matriarchal, and my aunt, mom and grandmother were tauruses, I grew up knowing which characteristics to embrace, which ones to shut t.f. down in public, and which ones to tweak when need be.

For over a decade, I've described myself as a unicorn, and if you decide to use the kinky definition of that, it's your prerogative, lol, but for the most part, I stick to the general definition: something or someone that's highly desirable but difficult to find or obtain. I've always been everywhere and nowhere completely unless I wanted to be. For a long time, I was a perfectionist.

I've been a straight A student my entire life, and because of that, do really well under pressure and take on challenges, face first. But it wasn't until I got my first B that I began dealing with failures. And yes, a B is a failure to me. I was valedictorian in kindergarten, delivering my first speech, and again in 5th grade, but in 8th grade, my world flipped upside down.

The F.E.W.:
DJ Kelly J, NotaboiDJ, Angie T

My mom moved us from Detroit, MI to Las Vegas, NV over the summer of 2003. My mom is a hustler's favorite hustler and can make a dollar appear out of thin air. My work ethic comes from her completely. She moved my baby sister, and I to Vegas for a better life. I didn't care about none of that shit. I had a new lil boyfriend and we had our first kiss, so I thought we were gonna get married, I had finally gotten popular, at the top of my school, not the class but the school, and was about to start high school at one of the big three: Cass, King, or Renaissance. Those were considered the top 3 high schools to attend in Detroit. You have to take a test AND score high to get into them, and my heart was set on Renaissance. But a "vacation" to Vegas to visit my favorite uncle and only father figure, turned into my mom letting me know that we were staying here, for good. I think I was upset for a couple years to be honest.

Detroit is predominately black. You drive to one suburb and maybe you'll see a few white people. Drive a little further out and you'll see a town of only middle eastern people. And the only Asian people you'll ever see, work at the Chinese restaurants or beauty supply stores. Vegas, whew... Vegas was the biggest culture shock

EVER. There were not a lot of black people, and the ones you could find were probably from California, which is home to a lot of interracial families. I've never seen so many variations of mixed people. I was confused seeing people that DEFINITELY were not 50% or more black using the N-word, and that was LAW in Detroit. I couldn't figure out what race most people were, and for safety purposes, it mattered. Vegas at the time was mostly white, even with all of the other races and mixtures of races here. Over the years, more talk of a minority majority emerged, but black people have always been the minority.

No part of my upbringing raised me to be comfortable around large groups of white people. I still look at the big scar on my right arm to this day of the girl that hit me with a cactus plant that rested on the check-in counter of an indoor playground I attended with family. My age is fuzzy, but I knew I was small, and she had told me that I couldn't play in the indoor playground because I was black. This was in the 90s, in the suburbs of Detroit, so this new place in 2003 was really scary to me. School was no longer fun, and the little bit of weight I had on me in Detroit was now full-on obesity in Vegas. My natural face wasn't acceptable either. Girls my age were already wearing makeup, and some were smoking cigarettes. What was even worse, is that I had teachers that barely spoke English. Yeah, my life was over. I got my first B and put myself on whatever kind of punishment I could conjure up at 13. It took time for me to like Vegas. It took even longer for me to love Vegas.

We were never rich, especially when we first moved to Vegas, but we were always okay because of my mom. I wanted to be rich though, lol. By 15, I had my first job at the New-York New York casino, stationed at a very busy coffee shop in the middle of the main floor. My mom helped me get my first car at 16. I got my first apartment at 18. I always wanted to make money, and always had a job, if not two or three.

By the time I was 18, I had two jobs, and I was over school. I still got really good grades. But the pressure to be perfect was fading. Finally. Part of it was self-inflicted. My grades weren't horrible, but there were a couple B's and C's. It would be so cold in class, that I would fall asleep before the bell to start class went off. My generation came right before the oh-so-wise generation of high school students that wore hoodies year-round. I found out shortly after that I have this on and off relationship with anemia. I had a weighed GPA of 3.71 and it was largely due to the AP classes I took. I vowed to NEVER let my child take AP classes. It had completely taken away every joy senior year is supposed to come with. I was ill prepared for prom, which was also in the same month of AP testing. My friends and I chipped in for a limo, so we could all ride together in style. But I was working til a few hours before we were supposed to meet up, and trying to get 6 people under the same schedule turned out to be a HOT mess. By the time it was all said and done, we arrived to our school's prom 5 minutes before it was over. We ran in with our dates to take photos, and that was it. Prom over. Senior year was this blur of being on the dance team, working, and struggling to stay awake and pass my AP classes.

I just KNEW I was going to be a doctor and would start with Nursing school. It was something my mom instilled in me when I was a kid, and I ran with it. I always wanted to help people. My grandmother had also moved to Vegas by this time. Her health has been a mess since before I was born. I have very few memories of her well. She was my best friend. Like, all the memes you see on social media of the grandparents with the candy in the purses, the soap opera lineups after school, that was MY grandma, lol. She was very feminine even when she wasn't well. She got her nails done faithfully every two weeks, had all the wigs you could imagine and the kinda sort a designer purse for every outfit. If I could help her and people like her, I'd have a sense of purpose.

My mom and I weren't extremely close, but I wasn't trying to leave her for college either. I got accepted into Clark Atlanta University and University of Nevada-Las Vegas. My research on colleges of choice was constantly interrupted by work and my AP classes. I was happy that I had these two, and ultimately chose to stay home in Vegas. Vegas had become home. UNLV it is! I toured the school and flaunted my UNLV apparel like I was on the basketball team or something, but the only "sport" I stuck with was dance. I was on the dance and step teams from sophomore year till senior year. I had been on somebody's dance team since I was 8, and it was the only creative space I felt I had.

The summer before starting college at UNLV, I was accepted for an internship at a local radio station. 88.1 FM KCEP. The general manager had come to one of my school's assemblies and mentioned a summer internship program there, the Bob Bailey Internship. A paid internship for high school graduates, allowing them to learn the ins and outs of radio. Once again, I was 18 and trying to make as much money as I could, and it seemed like a cool opportunity. It was a wrap. I was the only person that signed up from my school. Nobody could've told me that this internship would shift my life completely. I was supposed to be a doctor, start off as a nurse, and try to save the world. But I had left the internship with a fire in my heart, and a desire to do something different. To help people in a different way.

In the internship, you learn about EVERY position at a radio station. From the front desk, to accounting, to programming, to DJing, to operating the board, to being an on-air personality, every single position. It was there that I was introduced to DJing. It reminded me so much of the radio station I listened to in Detroit, WJLB. The on-air personalities were SO good, lol. I have never been a morning person, but I didn't miss their morning show before school. I remember all of the DJs names too. The main DJ here in Vegas, DJ Thump, used to leave his turntable setup for us to play around with during the internship. It was literally like my fingers were beginning to write a new story for my life the second they touched the turntables. I had at 18, accepted a new way to help people, with music.

So many DJs start off their stories with how much they love music, but I always felt like

The F.E.W.:
DJ Kelly J, NotaboiDJ, Angie T

EVERYBODY loves music. I haven't run into one person that ever said, "naaaah, I don't like any music."

I wanted to help people. And started this journey to be a DJ, to help people with music. Did I mention I dropped out of nursing school right before my state exams? The nursing program I had scholarships for…yeah…. my mom was PISSED. For what felt like some years. I've never been vocal, so I couldn't explain to her that I felt something special and have to follow it, no matter what. And I was scared of my momma! I'm 4 inches taller than her but have always feared her, lol. Communication with her was always really difficult. But I needed to do this, so I needed to figure out HOW to do this. Remember, I like money. Doctors make a lot of money. But how do DJs? Do they even make money? Did I just ruin my life?!

88.1 FM KCEP proved to be a home and family that I still have to this day. In my journey to make this decision make sense, I left the internship and went to another radio station. And another. And another. I learned about DJ coalitions, mixtapes, and such. Because of my dance background, I knew about all of the popular parties, and people. I was a part of a dance crew from senior year in high school till my early 20s, and we stayed outside after work or school. I started a position at an online radio station, which was decades before its time. It broadcasted all over the world and was funded by what appeared to be two but was really only one, wealthy man. Come to find out, he wasn't that wealthy either. I had two jobs there: one as a staff producer, a paid position where my role was to assist all of the existing radio shows on the station, and a non-paid position as an on-air personality. My time there is where I learned the local scene.

My radio show was geared toward young adults and aired every Saturday afternoon. I interviewed the best local artists, DJs, movers, and shakers, after researching my butt off on Myspace or word of mouth references. At the time, it was that or Blackplanet, lol. Facebook was out, but not really grabbing the young crowd as much. Things were going great there until one of my checks was late. Then another. Then a month went by and I still hadn't been paid. Then two, and some of the staff began to quit. Then... three. I loved being there SO much, but even at 19, I had bills, and not being paid in 3 months had me in a horrible bind. After going back and forth with my boss, I decided to leave the station, AND take legal action. It wasn't until another 3 months later that I was finally paid the money I was owed, but by then the damage was done.

After leaving that station, my navigation through the industry continued. I was hired as a street team member at 97.5 after meeting some of the DJs there at the parties I'd go to with my dance crew. One of them being DJ So Hype, who became one of my best friends over the years. 97.5 was the "poppin" station. If you worked there, you made it in Las Vegas as far as the urban market is concerned. But being on the street team was exactly the same as being an intern at 88.1, and I wanted more. I had been djing around town, building my name, and opening up for the experienced DJs. I had become Vegas' hottest female DJ by 2013, but to be clear, there were only maybe 4 female DJs at the time, lol.

I was tired of being on the street team, and ready to be on air. I kept reaching out to the program director at 97.5 about any audition opportunities for mixshow djs, but to no avail. Most times, she didn't respond to me at all. This itch inside of me to do more was driving me crazy; I felt stagnant. Me and stagnant don't do well.

DJ Thump was still someone I spoke with and vented to often, so I'm sure he made some magic happen. I received a phone call from him one day, telling me to send over a demo mix A.S.A.P. because some mixshow positions were opening at 88.1. Done! I made some new mixes and sent them over. Next thing I know, I was back at 88.1 this time with an on air mixshow position! It felt so good to be back, this time with a lot more experience. It truly felt like I was working with family; the chemistry was a complete 180 from 97.5. In my learning of the radio industry though, I learned that they functioned completely differently, too. At 88.1, we could break and interview local artists with little rebuttal. As long as the song was clean, and it "fit." But, the spins aren't tracked by BDS, a program that's used to scan songs played on registered radio stations. At 97.5, the spins are tracked by BDS, but good luck getting any local artist played on there. I was conflicted, because at my core, I wanted to help those dope artists I interviewed on my first radio show get through the door. In a couple years' time, I went back to 97.5 with a prime weekend mixshow slot, and then BACK to 88.1 with a prime slot. It had to have been pure luck that either station agreed to rehire me, but I did have a decent buzz around town. I was a really good DJ and had some support. 88.1 was so active in the community though, and what they offered won my heart at the end of the day. It was exactly how WJLB was in Detroit.

It was during this time that I met NotaboiDJ (I call her NAB, or by her real name, which she hates, lol) and Angie T (I call her Ang or by her real name, which she hates, lol). NAB reached out asking for mentorship, and honestly, I didn't think I knew enough to mentor anybody, deadass lol. I was cool with her shadowing me though. I had met a few female DJs by the time I met NAB, and I was irritated. I would be super eager to help them, only for them to quit after a couple of months, or the guys in the industry would immediately try to pin us against each other and do some kind of stupid DJ battle. DJ battles, especially in the city I call my second home, Las Vegas, make me cringe to this day. But NAB was different. She was from Chicago, and I sensed the Midwest in her immediately. Her work ethic was genuine, and she was dope from what I heard at the time. She reached out for mentorship, and she wasn't weird about it. I didn't want to compete with her, which was a brand-new reaction to a new female DJ in the city. I wanted to help her figure it out.

My introduction to Ang is blurry AF, and I don't know why, but I always remembered her being hilarious. In our few initial interactions, she was always stylish, funny, sharp, and very witty. I know where Kentucky is on a map but could never remember if it was considered the Midwest or the South, and Ang would some days sound like she's from the Midwest and some days sound like she's from the South, lol. Her energy was always dope, warm, and again, I sensed her work ethic was strong. Our radio family at 88.1 had grown to be this hilarious batch of people from all over, and over the years, NAB, Ang and I organically gravitated closer to each other both as friends, and co-workers, as events began to book us together. NAB would often work with me, especially after I had Z. And Ang began her brand as an on-air personality, which quickly extended to an event host/emcee. We've been stuck together, causing "necessary" trouble, ever since.

ANGIE T:

Angie T the Emcee in the place to be! Representing the Wind of The F.E.W, I am a Libra through and through. With the skills to balance out the most hectic situations with fair discernment but also will take 75 years to make a final decision. Charm comes natural and much like the wind I can go with the flow unless the flow goes against what I stand for and then I must tear it all down. A super power of mine is being able to start over. I'm on like my 3rd life right now but I do prefer to get things right the first time lol. Professionally I am a straight shooter. I can't stand fluff and I'm building my small talk portfolio because that's probably my least favorite thing to do. Don't get me wrong, I enjoy chatting and learning things about people. It's the dragged out, should've-ended-7 minutes-ago conversations where neither one of us knows how to wrap it up, kind of conversations that boils my chap! Give me the facts so I can make a balanced decision. I like to set clear expectations and lead with empathy. I'm the type of person that if we're friends today we are friends forever no matter how long it's been since we last talked. We will catch up. Loyalty, integrity & respect govern the type people I allow in my circle, but unfortunately in this industry you're going to come across a lot of pretenders so it's always good to put people where they should be in your life and DON'T PROMOTE THEM.

Born and raised in Louisville, KY I am 1 of 6 siblings plus 1 (long story, we'll talk about that in another book) hailing as the second oldest but I operate as thee oldest Queen B. Haha! My love for music started as a kid. My whole family either sang, played an instrument, produced music, or did a mix of all thee above. One of my most cherished memories is being back on the West side of Louisville on 18th & Date St at my family's church with my grandmother on piano, uncle on the organ, great grandmother in the pulpit, and my grandfather as the usher. My great grandfather led his classic Sunday morning song "Can't no boooody, do me like Jesus! Can't no booooody, do me like the Lord!" I can hear my mother's alto angelic voice singing with a tambourine with my siblings and I on the drums. As a kid, my siblings and I took turns playing the drums at church and I actually loved it. We low key were a family band now that I think about it. It's one of the things that brought us together.

The icing on the cake would be Sunday dinner after church, EVERYTHING was made from scratch. I can still remember sneaking into the kitchen at my grandmother's house and eating raw biscuit dough that was sitting in the fridge covered by a striped cloth.

Part of who I am is greatly attributed to the time & love my elders poured into me. Growing up, my grandparents and great-grandparents were my angels, offering me consistency, love, and sharing their own life lessons and experiences. I think about how we always joked with my great grandfather telling him he should've been a teacher because he would talk you right out of asking for whatever you were going to ask him for. It almost felt like it was only fair for him to say yes because I had been listening for 34 minutes, while my friends were outside waiting for me on their bikes in the driveway. He had just moved on to his third story about working in a warehouse back in the day, where a buddy of his got fired for stealing from the company. He emphasized the importance of independent thinking, reminding me that every action has a consequence. All I wanted was to ride my bike around the neighborhood. I could literally feel myself melting inside, waiting for it to end so I could go back to having fun and playing outside with my friends. In hindsight, I'd love to sit down and talk with him again <3

I didn't have everything I wanted but I had everything I needed. As you can imagine being raised primarily by your grandparents, I can smell a jive turkey from a mile away and I hate to waste. I come from a family of women leaders; my Great-grandmother was the leading heart of my family as a pastor. I always adored how people were captivated when she would speak. She would always tell me about the adversities she faced as a woman preacher coming up in the 60's. This helped me understand that, as a leader, you have to get things done by any means necessary— sometimes the soft, gentle approach just won't cut it. She and my great aunt (her daughter) would travel across the globe to speak at conventions, churches and classrooms. They weren't the type to tell you the same thing twice—so you had better listen up! Watching them, I knew it was only a matter of time before I found my voice and captivated the masses.

I love to work in groups. I believe there's power in unified numbers. As a kid I was in a singing group called the Luscious Ladies (hahaha gag right?) with me and 2 other members.

During my elementary and middle school years, I joined the cheer team and then moved to the step team in high school. However, from age 15 to 17, my high school years were pretty tough, and I missed out on a lot of traditional memories. While some people can reflect on milestones like prom, school dances, football games, and graduation, I can't.

To be honest, a big chunk of my teenage years was consumed by a runaway phase. In total, I was gone for maybe a little over a year. Crazy, right? I know. But we'll save that for the sequel. Still, it's those experiences that fuel my passion to always give back and connect with the younger generation. By my last year of high school, I was just focused on getting my diploma so I could get a job and move out of the city. I always knew that whatever life had in store for me was beyond Louisville's city limits. Not to say success couldn't be achieved there, it just wasn't part of my personal quest. I was over the whole high school experience and ready to be grown. I was determined to see it through, especially since my grandfather promised to buy me a car as a graduation gift. Chile, I GOT IT DONE! I didn't even attend my graduation because, honestly, it didn't feel necessary or important. Most of the people I went to school with had graduated the year before, and after attending four different high schools, I didn't really know any of the students anyway.

I was busy trying to formulate a plan on how I was going to move to Cincinnati, OH! As I mentioned I was looking for a way to get away and start anew. At the time, my then boyfriend lived in Cincinnati as well so it felt like an easy choice. I started filling out applications online for a job that would pay me enough to handle my bills. After about a month of applying online with my spruced-up resume from my customer service experience, I was able to start my career in Accounting!

The funny thing is, I had no real idea what the job would entail. I just knew it was an office position that offered training, was located in Downtown Cincinnati, and paid well. And the cherry on top? It was Black-owned, a surprise I didn't even discover until after I was hired! About a month or so after moving there with him, I had found my own apartment and at that point you couldn't tell me nothing! 19, no kids, car paid off, apartment, a man, and a good job! I stayed there a little over 4yrs before moving back home to KY after my grandmother passed, but boy I had a TIME! During my time there, I formed lifelong bonds with people I still keep in touch with today. I was introduced to a different kind of love, and Cincinnati will always be my second home.

My career in the entertainment industry has been quite the experience. I still remember the moment I decided I was going to move to Vegas. It was right after I wrapped up my fourth tax season, working as a tax preparer, brand ambassador, and marketing rep. This was also after winning the Ms. Lady Liberty beauty pageant. As Ms. Liberty, I became the face of the Louisville chapter. Now, I know this might sound fancy, but baby, this pageant took place at Newburg Park. Not that it's a bad park, but I'm just saying, they were making the best of it! Would you believe me if I told you I won that pageant by remixing 'Rapper's Delight' into an anti-bullying song. Chile I looked like Michelle Obama mixed with MC Lyte. I loved the role! I was a double threat because it allowed me to learn and teach people about taxes. Then I could switch it up, put on my dress and crown and go do community work. Sometimes I'd go to the schools or libraries to read to the kids in full beauty pageant glam. I'd attend local events to network or I'd be living my best life at the festivals on our floats waving to everyone passing out goodies. I was able to partner up with other writers and comedians to co-write & produce four tv-broadcasted commercials for the brand. I literally had never felt liberated like that in a work space where my creativity had no limit. Chile, we even remixed "No Flex Zone by Rae Sremmurd and made a song called "No Discount Zone." It was unorthodox and freaking brilliant! It was this work experience that let me know I wanted to be a part of something like that all year round. It was also a life lesson that if you put your best foot forward in everything you do you literally have no idea where it can take you!

So, I decided I would visit a friend that lived in Vegas. I wanted to go to Cali but I didn't know anyone there and I knew it would be way more expensive being solo so I went to the next best thing. Before visiting Vegas I had my own agenda in mind. I wanted to visit radio stations, media companies and networking events. ALL OF IT! I was determined to make a connection that would get me to Vegas. I stayed in Vegas for 2 weeks going full force. I went to an open mic where I met DJ Cool. I told him about my plans to come to Vegas to pursue media, and he mentioned that he was starting a radio show here in Vegas and was looking for a female radio host. I JUMPED at the opportunity! Didn't ask a lot of questions, I just knew I could pivot and start anew.

About 2 weeks after returning back to home, I lost a little bit of steam from the Vegas trip not to mention I kind of balled out while there by going 4 wheeling, fine dining, car rental, shopping etc., so I started looking for a job in Louisville and set up my second interview at a CPA firm ready to get back on the hamster wheel. DJ Cool ended up calling me back "Yo Angie it's DJ Cool, I'm seeing if you are still interested in doing the radio show. I just got the green light and we're ready to take off in 2 weeks." I. Was. Stunned! Like ohhh he was for real for real! Ha! Welp God if this is my sign I'm jumping ship and I expect you to catch me.

With a 2-week notice, I moved to Vegas, baby I gassed up my little 2001 Mazda 6, packed as much as I could in my car and hit the road with my friend Joe. Joe, by the way, is one of those forever friends. He was actually at work when I called him frantically "Joe omg! I can't believe the person who was supposed to drive with me to Vegas canceled last minute and I'm scared to drive alone!" Without taking a breath he replied, "Don't worry I got you, I'm going to leave work, just get my arrangements to come back and we good." And just like that, we hit the road, with my check engine light on and everything. Whew! The ghettooooo! I do not recommend by the way. But God's grace is everything because we made it in 24 hours straight!

Working on the 'West Wit It' radio show was a great experience. DJ Cool was very patient in training me on the mic and allowing my personality to shine through. He's actually the one who gave me my stage/radio name Angie T. I started there and moved to a different show I produced on Vegas Raw Radio, where I was determined to have my own sound. My co-host were McKinley, Sharon, Random ass dude and DJ tonearms would spin for us. I loved this cause baby we weren't getting paid a dollar for it, but we had passion and drive to see it through. I would attend events in the community and network the best I could.

I'll never forget when I first saw Kelly J upon moving to Vegas. I came out to network and get familiar with the community. It was like I literally saw this girl at EVERY EVENT. I was thinking, "Who is this superwoman?! I got to meet her." I even had Kelly J come on my internet radio show. I went through loops to get her but we made it happen with the help of our mutual friend, Sharon. So, when we ended up being at the same station I knew we'd be locked in. Meeting NAB, she came in to DJ on the show Simply T and I did on Friday nights at KCEP. I thought she was a little "too friendly" and always smelled like candy. I had to be sure there wasn't any ulterior motives before letting her in because why do you smell so sweet? Are you trying to distract me? Lol God's timing is everything.

And that my friends is, "The F.E.W.." Now it's game time...

TRACK 1:
Bitch Better Have My Money
Demanding Your Worth

DJ Kelly J:

A ng and I had left 88.1 but were still working heavily with NAB, and we were on the prowl for a space to do our own events together. We stumbled across a venue, we'll call it Club A. Club A was in a decent location, had bomb food and a good track record for paying DJs on time, which is an ongoing issue in the industry everywhere. I scheduled a meeting with the owner/manager (people are always lying about their true positions, idk) to go over logistics. NAB came with me to meet the owner/manager and check out the place. We weren't the FEW just yet but agreed to work together on as many projects as possible, with Club A being the first opportunity.

The booking rates for DJs and Hosts vary from place to place, and depend on SO many details, such as experience, ability to promote and/or bring a crowd, and actual skill level. In nightlife, your ability to negotiate determines your pay, as nightlife tends to pay the least out of the different entertainment avenues, unless you're a major artist/DJ. Honestly, even they negotiate rates.

Most people have managers or agents that handle the negotiations for them, but we were in a stage of learning how to handle these things on our own.

At this point in my career, I could easily negotiate rates for myself, but trying to negotiate rates for the F.E.W. was challenging...as hell. We had started our careers at different times, and locally, it was easier for me to get into certain doors with just my resume. I had full faith in the movement we were creating together and wanted us to make moves collectively. The owner/manager wanted me to take over certain days there weekly, and I negotiated a higher rate than most DJs on the roster there, just enough to split the pay equally with the F.E.W. It was a great rate for one person, but still wasn't that great for three people.

NAB:

This was a wonderful opportunity but on top of us needing to DJ and bring all of our equipment to the venue, we were expected to promote the night as well. A lot of places expect talent to promote the night that they're working, without having a budget for it or a discussion outlining these expectations. (WHY DO YALL DO THAT?) We usually get the short end of the deal and are tricked into pushing these nights because we genuinely want to come out successful and obtain a residency. The worst thing when doing business is to NOT have a contract, which we didn't. This was a huge revelation when it came to this night which we called, "Afrobeat Vibes" (IYKYK). When you're putting together a DJ contract, you gotta make sure all the details are tight. Start with the basics: the date, time, location, and break down exactly what you're supposed to do – like how long you're spinning and what gear you need. Get the money stuff clear: how much you're getting paid, when you're getting the deposit, and when the rest is due. Don't forget to lay out the cancellation rules – what happens if either side pulls out. Food and beverages is a key component that you don't want to forget to add. There's no reason you should be working at an establishment and be starving or dying of thirst. Not cool! Cover your back with some liability insurance for any damage or drama that might pop off. And of course, make sure both sides sign and date that bad boy to seal the deal. This was a weekly event that we attempted to make our own by djing, promoting, naming, coming up with specials, etc. Oh, and there are specific rules when it comes to licensing which stated that they weren't allowed to have a dance floor so it was difficult when trying to encourage people to dance. Who knew? SMH

Angie T:

I was there, but because we have done so many events, my memory is slightly blurry on the details. But I trusted Kelly J and NAB had this covered... lol NEXT!

NAB:

OH yes Angie T, yo ass was definitely there:

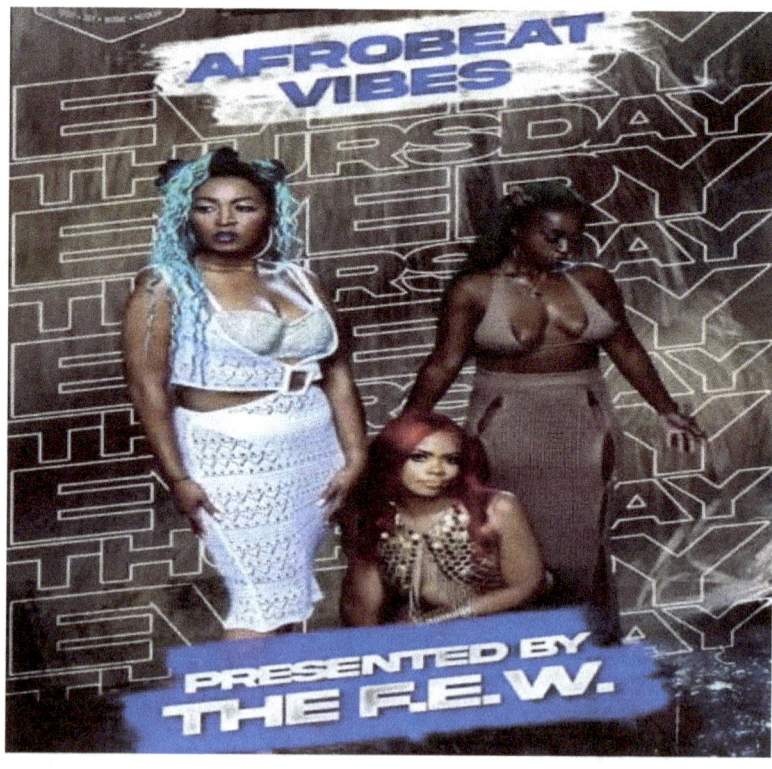

The F.E.W.:
DJ Kelly J, NotaboiDJ, Angie T

Kelly J:

Afrobeat Vibes" Thursday nights with the F.E.W. was hit or miss, although we had only been running for a couple months so far. Ultimately, Thursdays ended abruptly, and I was left with just Friday nights, with the ability to bring in guest DJs here and there. NAB and Ang would alternate working with me on Fridays –

NAB – We did!?!

Kelly J:

Girl hush! It's my turn! Anyway... NAB and Ang would alternate working with me on Fridays as they both began getting other work on Friday nights. Club A was consistent, but there was a salary cap in place, and for some reason, payments were starting to come late. Red flag. There was no contract, which was the norm for most clubs and lounges like this, and communication was starting to get really choppy, which was another red flag. My anxiety started kicking in, as well as both NAB and Ang expressing their concerns, so when the offer came to go to Club B, a place where I had no payment issues, AND I was getting paid way more, I dipped. I let Club A know of my departure, and they were pissed, but I was excited to be back in a spot that I trusted, kinda.

This was my second time at Club B, with the first time being the very lucrative opportunity to be a promoter, which I'll talk about in the Self-Discipline chapter. I don't mention how it ended: there was an altercation in the parking lot one night, a night that a different promoter was running. Someone started shooting, and although nobody was hurt, the club was within a probationary period, in which they could have no issues in order to obtain their permanent license to operate fully. Because of this shooting, their license was revoked completely, and Club B was shut down.

This had become the fate of various urban lounges and nightclubs in Las Vegas, and although it was my first experience of this as a promoter, it was maybe my 3rd or 4th including places I Dj'ed for. It left an extremely sour taste in my mouth. Working so hard to build something for months, having it become successful, then it ending abruptly because of something someone else did was the most irritating shit I've ever felt.

Club B was closed for a little over a year before it reopened, under a new name and new management. One of the previous owners was still there and called me personally one night. He mentioned that Club B had returned and was looking for assistance with rebranding it. My track record from before served as my resume, and both owners were able to see my consistent sales that spread over 10 months. The previous owner explained my following to the new owner, which I still call to this day, "sophisti-ratchet." Basically, a combination of educated entrepreneurs, activists, rappers, singers, models, socialites and partygoers, with minimal riff raff. I never had so much as a scuffle on my nights before, and they needed THAT kind of crowd in there.

I had a three-month salary contract to DJ, in which I still designed the flyers and promoted a little bit. I don't like when work feels like work, and that's what DJing in the same place 4 days a week was starting to feel like. I wasn't excited to spin, and on top of that, the new co-owner wasn't familiar with entertainment at all. What was a bit of abuse of power, and pissing me off, he would try to reduce my pay over minor things. None of that was in the contract, and I was so glad I had one this time. The previous owner had been in entertainment for over a decade, but this new co-owner was brand new, and all over the place with management, communication, and assuming that a nightlife business is run exactly like any other business. In Vegas, that's a huge mistake. As the entertainment capital in the Wild Wild West, a lot of rules, laws and licenses are very unique to just this city.

When my contract was up, we mutually agreed that I'd go down to one day a week, with the opportunity to promote as I did before. I opted to still DJ on their other nights if they needed me, but under a flat rate with a set amount of hours. I immediately offered to bring the F.E.W. in, with a chance to try out our Afrobeat night, this time with the name, "Rhythm & Beats."

The F.E.W.:
DJ Kelly J, NotaboiDJ, Angie T

NAB:

Club B was quite challenging due to its management or lack thereof and the energy that the venue held. We started there without a contract and why we did that, I for one will never know. It quite consistently had a different group of customers that would frequent the place which made our sets complex. We were supposed to only play Afrobeat with R&B but always had requests of Rap or Trap music which was supposed to be a NO-NO. I mean if they weren't tipping I didn't have a problem with telling them no. IJS, if you are asking a DJ to play your song then you need to come correct AKA with cash. If you didn't know, now you do. Like who raised you mfs? We were once again put in a position where we had to promote this night and try to get people to come. There were nights when we would show up and the club would still be closed, the chef wasn't there, and nobody knew nothing. A HOT MESS.

Eventually we addressed the fact that we didn't have a contract and we were told that they wouldn't do a contract instead they'd give us an agreement..*WHHHHAAAAATTT*. Attempt after attempt, but we kept getting the runaround which left us tired and defeated. I told "The F.E.W." that they could go on without me because I needed a contract to continue (Fuck a damn agreement)!

Angie T:

As I mentioned before, I have always been down for a good time, but when the money gets funny, it's time to roll, lol! Honestly, I can't remember the details of this either. I just know I show up when I'm supposed to and leave when it ain't right. I'm taking flight!

Kelly J:

Although NAB decided to leave, and Ang shortly after, I stayed at Club B to ride it out, unsure if I was making the right decision or not. I was given a residency agreement as a promoter and once again, began the challenge of building up my night. It was a lot harder than before, a LOT harder. The scene was so much different after COVID, and honestly things never got back to how it was before.

Along with making sure people were there consistently, it was more and more important that the RIGHT people were in there this time. I brought back one of my resident DJs, DJ Blahze, and to ensure everyone got paid on time, I didn't have as many guest DJs. It was just me and him for AWHILE until he had to make a sudden exit. I switched him out with another longtime friend of mine, King Smash. Me and this co-owner had bumped heads a handful of times before an incident occurred that shifted our relationship. After over 3 months, we had finally reached a night where the guestlist RSVPS were nonstop, and the club was going to be full. Yes laaawd! Early that day, the owners of Club B received a call from licensing, demanding that they shut down due to some stipulation that I'm convinced somebody made up THAT DAY. Both owners called me saying we had to shut down, hours before we were to open. I don't even know why I was so calm. They were frantic, the co-owner kept ranting about how much money he lost investing in the club already, and the tone of his voice was something to the effect of "I've lost EVERYTHING." But I was so calm. I was running around with Z and my boyfriend at the time, and all I remember is saying, "We're going to open tonight." I told them to hold off on posting that we would be closed on social media, then proceeded to call and text ALL of my politician friends for help.

Because of my many years of community work, I personally know a lot of local politicians. I called and texted every single one of them until I got a solution. I try to learn as much as I can outside of entertainment, but to be honest there's a LOT to master in entertainment first. Some days I can't tell you what I ate, let alone what law is what, so having a relationship with politicians I could call for help proved to be a lifesaver time and time again. In this case, the politician told me to give him a little while, so that he could personally call the licensing department. Whew, the powers that be didn't like that, lmao! My politician friend called me back a few hours later stating that Club B could purchase something like an add on to their license, and that we could open that night. The co-owner, who was working my last nerve, all of a sudden wanted to be besties. He mentioned the dissatisfaction of whomever called him initially when they called back to inform him of the politician's call. The relief in his voice was so hard to not laugh at. They purchased the add-on, and we had a successful night, finally. It was at this point that I no longer faced rebuttal in my pay or conditions at Club B. Anything that I asked for within reason, I got.

After about 2 more months, Club B was starting to feel like the good ole days. My night was consistently busy, and I started bringing in special guests to DJ or host again. I brought back my featured showcases spotlighting upcoming artists and cross promoted them on large radio platforms while still filling up the club. Our busiest night thus far, was our last though. I was exhausted, after doing back-to-back gigs, and Z had just started pre-k. Being out til 3am then getting up at 7am to feed her and get her ready for school was kicking my butt, even with the help of my mom and boyfriend. The club that night was full early, it was barely 11pm. I arranged with King Smash that I'd head out early, get Z and take my butt to bed, and for him to finish out the night.

I got a call around 1am saying that I needed to return back to the club immediately. Half awake, I murmured, "Why, what happened?" The co-owner informed me of a shooting that happened outside, near the parking lot. The police came, and shut the club down. My heart dropped. Although nobody got hurt, thank God, something happened on MY night. My promoter's license was on the line, and once again, the club was in their probationary period. I had Z and couldn't leave her, so I couldn't return to the club, and I was immediately informed that the promoter is to remain on the premises for the full duration of the event. Damn! The pesky co-owner had one up on me and wasn't letting down at all. I always found it funny that society deems women as the overly emotional ones, but I have MANY memories of men losing it more than women. It's not that women are more emotional, or that men are, but that WE BOTH are. We're human and therefore, imperfect and emotional. Men in a male-dominated industry get to have a way with the narrative though, lol. Anywho, in this human experience, it was this co-owner's time to shine!

In this conversation with him, he blamed me for getting the club shut down, even after the strings I pulled to help keep it open before. Trying to stay calm through all of the b.s. coming my way via phone AND text, I backed down. In the final verbal exchange, I finished with, "You're right. Good luck with trying to fix this one." I think that set him off more. But I was exhausted, and through all the precautions taken to get a good crowd there, this incident, that I had no control of, STILL happened and my license was affected. This extremely high risk was a gamble I wasn't willing to take again. The money wasn't enough, and I realized that I didn't have the time flexibility that I thought I did, so I took a hard break from promotions. I went back to solely djing, while I barely wiggled through this loss. It was a few months later that an offer from Club C came.

Club C proved to be a testament of our resilience, and newfound growth as a brand. Although we were independently working on things, collectively our brand had become a beast. This was the first spot that was eager to book the three of us with no bite back for the most part. We had a 6-month residency together; Saturdays belonged to "The F.E.W.".

NAB would DJ Saturday evenings and I had Saturday mornings, with Ang hosting. We were matched in terms of pay and even had a marketing budget. Club C belonged to whom I call the G.O.A.T.'s of the city; their track record doubled mine and they played an integral role in the urban entertainment culture. I was beyond excited to be working with them and to be building the brand of "The F.E.W." with their support.

NAB:

We met in October at Club C to discuss "The F.E.W. 's" collaboration with the goals that they had in place. The discussion was about doing a DJ battle, concerts, and their nightly events for the upcoming year. The DJ battle was going to be for the Juneteenth festival where there would be DJ Kelly J & I going back and forth in a battle. I swiftly expressed that I was uninterested in battling so instead they called it "dueling" DJs. We were going to circle back to that event since it was so far out, but like many other things, that never happened. Then they proceeded to discuss the upcoming concert in which New Edition would be the headliner. The F.E.W. was beyond ecstatic with the opportunity to be a part of such a significant show being held in Las Vegas. Angie T wanted tickets to the concert, DJ Kelly J offered to assist and promote in any way possible, I wanted to open and DJ for the concert. We got NONE! Going over the contract was something that needed to happen a few times before we could start. There were a lot of errors and absolutely no mention of our drink or food comps which is a must. After a few weeks, they got it together and we were off to our new endeavor! Sidenote: Roughly 3 months later, I got to open up for the New Edition concert with a collaboration that this venue's promoters had with 88.1 which is the radio station that I work at. Won't he do it!!!

Club C became our home. They paid for us to have a photoshoot, posted flyers, and promoted us thoroughly. We were knee deep in that shit too. Our TikToks were designed to make everyone come and see The F.E.W. at the hottest new black owned spot in Las Vegas. Guess what? They did! It took literally no time for people to start pouring in and turning up with us. Now the bad thing about this venue is that the service was hella slow and the food was inconsistently good and bad. Every week there was a new chef who had a new recipe for the same food and BABY it was a hot mess. Orders were not only slow af but they weren't even trying to accommodate people for their fuck ups, like

The F.E.W.:
DJ Kelly J, NotaboiDJ, Angie T

Bruhhhhhh. Just so you know, when we have gigs, that does not make us liable for the mishaps that they have within the establishment.

New Year's came and I was booked to DJ until midnight. It was sold out, so people were packed in there like Mexicans trying to bring in their New Year at a spot that was conveniently not placed on the strip in Las Vegas. When the clock struck 12, I said my "Happy New Year's" to everybody, gave my hunty a kiss, and was GONE. The next day I saw that the owner had called me because there was some miscommunication and he expected for me to DJ until later since the party was still turnt. DJ Kelly J called me to admonish my behavior by saying that I should have just stayed since it was New Years. I was booked until 12 so that's when my gig is up! I like to stand on business. This ain't the first and won't be the last time that "The F.E.W." doesn't see eye to eye, but it is what it is.

As time went on, eventually, our contract was coming to an end and needed to be renegotiated. The collaboration was going pretty good and the hiccups were slowly coming to a halt so we were eager to continue our agreement with Club C. However, there was little to no response from the owners about renewing our contract and time was running out. Eventually, I decided to end our partnership for lack of an agreement that would outline everything that I requested but DJ Kelly J and Angie T kept working with them. Although, in the near future 88.1 radio station had secured a weekly residency at Club C in which my presence was requested. So, I actually returned for this opportunity because I know working with the radio station that my bread will come like clockwork. Fortunately, by then, the service and food had vastly improved!

Kelly J:

Waittttt a minute now. Technically, I became a rotating guest DJ; they never offered me another residency. Ang stayed. Okay go head Ang!

Angie T:

Now when Club C came into the picture, it was actually quite on time! I remember telling Kelly J and NAB I was trying to venture out of the night club scene to something different. I mean don't get me wrong, I'm down for a good time, but if we could get it done before 6pm and I have the rest of the day to myself, then I'm game. Besides, I loved the idea they had for us and felt we deserved this considering all the things we had just experienced. I remember sitting at the table and discussing the dueling DJ set which I was excited for, and overall, the respect as professionals was appreciated. Starting out, I remember it was slow. We had like 12 people show up and 5 of them worked there. Nonetheless, we made sure to show them a good time, which rewarded us in the long haul because those same people are now a part of the packed house we have each weekend.

This was a pivotal moment in my hosting and emcee career because it was a sustainable offer that gave me creative freedom. Plus, it's a residency, which means consistency. I truly respect and appreciate them for bringing the offer to us/me. I was starting to lose hope in finding viable opportunities as an emcee/host. Unfortunately, hosting and being an emcee can sometimes be undervalued, even though it's truly an art. And once you learn your value, that's where the real challenge comes into play—because you're no longer doing it just for fun or experience. Now, you've got a packaged product and a respectable brand, so pay me! We all came to the table and signed our separate agreements. When it came time to renew the contract, I moved forward based on a verbal agreement to continue the same agreement. Let's be clear—I'm not recommending anyone do this, because it often doesn't end well, or at the very least, it leaves you unprotected if issues arise. At that point, you're operating on verbals, and let's be honest—people say all kinds of sh*t and act like they never said it when it no longer benefits them. For me, it was more of a 'lets see where this goes' kind of situation. If the venue and I decided to part ways for any reason, then so be it—PEACE OUT. By this point, I had mastered the art of detaching and pivoting.

Mind you, this was extra income on top of everything else I had going on, so I could sustain myself either way. Plus, I genuinely loved doing it. I looked forward to every weekend, so I didn't feel the need to push the issue. I trusted the owner to keep his word, and as long as they upheld their end of the bargain, I'd continue giving my 100%. I wasn't a fan of not being able to continue with my girls, but I also didn't have a say. We talked about it. My girls wished me well and, we continued to work together outside of Club C of course so it didn't stop our flow. Before long, Club C was impressed with my work and asked if I wanted to bring my energy to an additional day. This is an example of how sometimes in the industry, you can take a chance and still come out on top. I don't regret a thing. It was this opportunity that was pivotable in my Emcee/Host career and from that point baby the price went UP (again).

The F.E.W.:
DJ Kelly J, NotaboiDJ, Angie T

Kelly J:

Two things can be right, I think, lol. NAB was right in demanding that terms were made clear to her beforehand, and since they weren't, she was out at 12 on the dot. I tried to explain to her though, that New Years Eve and New Years Day are two of the most impulsive days for any venue, and that although they should have communicated a possible extension of time beforehand, cutting ANY party exactly at midnight, and especially on New Years Eve is crazy! It's another case-by-case thing, as NAB's relationship with that venue isn't the same as my relationship with that venue.

Relationships, and communication, play a really big role in the entertainment industry.

Angie T:

Yeah I think honestly people have to learn who to play with lol some people bend and some stand on the business agreement. Speaking of which, Kelly J, remember when the business damn near ran us over?

Kelly J:

There was one situation where a lack of communication proved to wave ALL of the red flags we needed to leave a work opportunity, and we didn't do so til the day of.

The three of us were still in the middle of our residency at Club C and were allowing the momentum of the F.E.W. brand to flow freely. We had just finished our photoshoot and began working on our EPK and joint social media pages. We were still working on the consistency of things, while balancing personal matters and our independent brands. I was doing my routine scrolling on IG and came across a page promoting an event for Grammy Awards weekend in southern California. I saw an opportunity and went for it. I messaged their IG, promoting the idea of an all-female trio, 2 DJs and one emcee, to open for the event, sending over a few links of our work together so far. They actually responded and accepted the offer! I got the number of a guy that told me he was the organizer of the event. I did a bit of research on him and the event, but I definitely should've done more....

We had a call the day after, going over all the possibilities, and I immediately called NAB and Ang about the opportunity. NAB wasn't playing any games about us doing this gig without a contract. We put together a contract for him to sign, requesting our fee and hotel stay covered for us to head that way. He signed, we signed, and we made our arrangements for the trip.

We were supposed to get a deposit before we EVER left Las Vegas. The lack of communication began, and the date he told us we'd receive our deposit kept being pushed further and further away. It's now the day of, and the guy tells us we'd get it at soundcheck. Yikes. At this point, celebrities were booked and confirmed to be at the event. Excited about the opportunity, we still began our journey to California, with NAB flying out there, and Ang and I driving in our own cars. Ang and I were about 2 hours out, NAB was already there on the beach, and communication was getting worse with no solid details of our hotel room. The guy stops responding to the calls and texts, with a final text sending the number of his "assistant" who was going to get the hotel information for us. Laaawd. I was irritated AF and started to feel sick. We were determined to have this dope night and wanted to see it through, hot mess and all. The assistant says that we need to meet with another guy, a much older man, to get our hotel information. I was ready for some wine immediately. Where TF did this old man come from and why are we getting our hotel rooms from him?! Now that I think about it, I think he was the assistant's sugar daddy or something, cause what the hell?!

The F.E.W.:
DJ Kelly J, NotaboiDJ, Angie T

There's no turning back now, so we continued the drive to Hollywood.

NAB:

Now when DJ Kelly J brought me & Angie T on board for the California gig during Grammys week, you couldn't tell me nothing. I'm like, "Mama we made it!" because this was my first out of state gig so I was getting all the way together. I bought a new outfit, hired a makeup artist, canceled other gigs, and booked my flight. DJ Kelly J and Angie T were driving their cars but me doing my own thing is quite common, plus I needed to go to the beach once I got there for spiritual alignment and didn't need anyone else's itinerary getting in my way. Let's just say, I'm SO glad I made it to mami wata!

Once I arrived at the airport, I ubered straight to the beach. There was constant communication between myself and "The F.E.W." about our room accommodations, the deposit, which had not been received, and the events. It was like there was no way to really get the serenity that I was seeking because it was nonstop calls, emails, and texts. All of a sudden, one of us needed to get to the hotel ASAP to check in with some random old pilgrim that none of us knew to get the keys. "Like where the hell did this old ass Caucasian man come from." The hotel was like 3 hours from the beach in Cali traffic, and I was the closest since DJ Kelly J and Angie T were still driving. I hit my homie that was in town for the events that I had invited him to, and he told me to Uber half way because with the traffic, we still wouldn't make it in time. When I tell you I spent so much money on rides within the 1st hour of arriving; I was hella irritated. Once we met up, he got me to the hotel to meet the guy that was already gone but they still allowed me to check in (Thank God). The hotel was beautiful, everyone was super nice, and they had a restaurant with a bar. Yup, I needed food and drinks cuz I was not feeling spiritually tapped in at all so I was all too eager to indulge in the spirits they had to offer.

There was an event that night in which we were scheduled to be at with the expectations that there would be VIP seats waiting for us. The devil is a lie and the truth ain't in him cuz we didn't have not 1 seat. I paid a make-up artist to beat my face, we wore matching outfits, and just knew that it was going to be a spectacular night. Let me tell you that the exact opposite happened that night including us running around trying to find the promoter who hired us. There were bands performing that were pretty dope but the sound in the venue was trash, there were NO seats for us, and it was freezing.

The F.E.W.:
DJ Kelly J, NotaboiDJ, Angie T

Now the heels that I wore were contingent upon us being able to sit down, so I was ready to go as soon as chairs weren't an option. We stayed long enough to take pics, then we left!

The next day, I had to go back to the beach to get my mind right. There was a beautiful restaurant on the beach in Malibu, so Angie T and myself made our way there because I needed my spiritual healing again. Everything about that experience was amazing. I said my prayers, touched the water, and did some offerings. Angie T and I even found time for us to make a quick lil TikTok while we were there.

Later that night, we were scheduled to perform but still hadn't received a deposit for our services. I had already booked a makeup artist again, so here I am all cute and dressed up with nowhere to go. Yup, you guessed it! Not only did we not get a deposit, we got ghosted. Now the frustrating part is that this was DJ Kelly J's connect so she was the middle man and we didn't have much say in how the night transpired. She basically told us what was texted and that he wasn't holding up his end of the deal...THE END. You can get the rest of the story from the other members of the group cuz that shit had me pissed and I'm done talking about it.

On the brighter side, we were all going our separate ways on Sunday but there was some light at the end of the tunnel. I have a cousin that works with a few DJ's back in Chicago who just so happened to be coming to Cali for some Grammy events. Crazy thing is I needed to get back to Vegas to do a gig that I had already committed to, and I definitely couldn't afford to miss any money after this weekend's shenanigans. So off I went to the airport to be a responsible adult butttttt...I told Angie T if she wanted to stay, then I would come back so that we could go to the event and my cousin would let us crash at their spot. Whole time, DJ Kelly J had come to Cali with her boyfriend so they kinda had their own itinerary. Angie T was game, which applied hella pressure to ya girl. I legit flew my ass back to Vegas, DJ'd, and flew back to Cali all in the same day so we could make it to the festivities that night. Sidenote...I kept my expensive ass makeup on from the day before so I was flyyyyyyyy. We got to see DJ Kid Capri & DJ Terry Hunter at the same party which made all of the foolishness that happened not seem so bad. I mean that shit was still bogus, but we tried to make the best of it. In this industry NOTHING is a guarantee; We have been through a lot together, but we've always been able to maintain our friendship. I hope you've been taking notes and learning some shit cuz you best believe we did!!!

Angie T:

California baby! That was something! I still remember being in the hotel room waiting on NAB to finish her makeup so we could go to sound check and we get the text from Kelly J that the promoter wasn't paying us, so the show was off. It felt like time stood still! I was confused. I was mad. I was not understanding how we got here?! I wanted to pull up to the venue so we could talk in person cause ain't no way these people paid for our room accommodations and created a flier for them to just decide not to have us perform and not pay us. But before I could gather the girls, Kelly J followed up and said she went up there and the promoter didn't come to the door. I was even more confused AND mad! Like whaaaat?! But you know that was probably God's plan, cause if I would have went up there, in the words of Denzel Washington, "I'm leaving here with SOMETHING!" I remember looking at NAB like "Well… What do we do now?" At first we started to look up other events and things to do and then came to the conclusion that we were hungry so guess what. Room service, baby! We ate GOOD that night! We had steak, pizza, wine, subs, sandwiches, appetizers and more. We had the homie in Cali pull up, place his order and we kicked it on the balcony chopping it up before retiring to bed. Breakfast was just as grand! If I wasn't getting paid I was going to eat my pay.

Now the next day was a different story. Honestly my spirit was not content with leaving Cali on that sour note so when NAB told me her family was coming into town to have a Grammy party I was so down to just have fun & network. Afterall, somebody needed to see how cute I was. The party in Hollywood was all that and a bag of chips! It was held in an art gallery, with beautiful Black art displayed everywhere. There was a spiraling staircase that led to an overlooking balcony, and everyone had on their Sundays best. The atmosphere was definitely grown and sexy. We had such a great time. It was dope to see DJ Kid Kapri in action as an emcee and DJ. He ROCKED THE CROWD! I remember telling NAB this is the kind of set I wanted to do. I previously tried to describe it to her so it was perfect for us to see it in person together. He had us in a headlock the whole time he was on the tables. You'd thought it was a concert. I think for half a second NAB actually allowed herself to have fun. We danced on the dance floor, took our pictures, and made some connections along the way. Sometimes things don't go as planned, so you either look at the glass half full or break that mf!

Kelly J:

This sh*t had me sick to my stomach, literally. Knowing that everyone took off work and made accommodations to be out here, AND we didn't get paid, on something I brought to the table, was heartbreaking. What's the point of having a contract if nobody cares to follow it?! This guy gave zero cares about screwing us over, and worse, was trying to talk us out of the contract we signed. By this time, I'm full on nauseous, unsure if it's the circumstances of this event or something else but needed a solution ASAP. We were less than an hour prior to our soundcheck time, with no deposit. I didn't want NAB or Ang to deal with it, so after trying to deal with it myself, to no avail, I told them we weren't going to set up for the event tonight. I think if things went differently in the trip beforehand with this event organizer, and especially if he paid the deposit at least, I would've suggested that we go set up. But I genuinely didn't trust this guy anymore, and wasn't about to have us working for free, or in any weird situations. He never sent anything, didn't care, and thought we came to just kick it. Nah, we're not setting foot in there, let alone setting up. I'm glad NAB and Ang had the time to enjoy the weekend in California; I had to hurry back home, get to a gig, and figure out what was going on with my body internally. Needless to say, I felt shitty about it all for AWHILE. My main issue with verbal communication is people can make up whatever they want and change their stories with no evidence unless you're recording a conversation. Then the he-said, she/they-said war begins. Text messages and emails ALWAYS leave receipts. To this day, I get cringey about any business matters done verbally. Those memes where people text someone, but if the person calls, they watch the phone ring then continue to text them, that's me in a LOT of situations. We also saw that contracts

The F.E.W.:
DJ Kelly J, NotaboiDJ, Angie T

hold less power than we may think, and entertainment lawyers are needed in some cases.

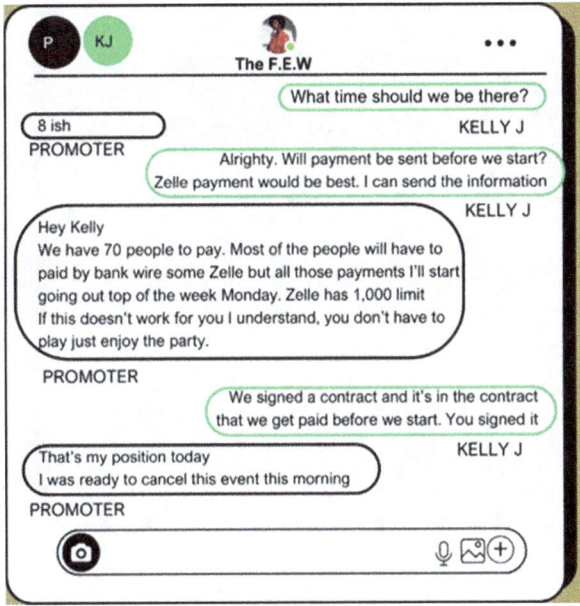

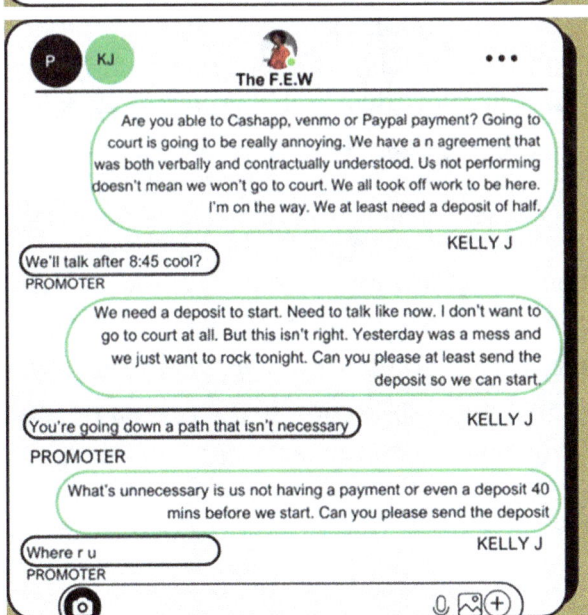

NAB:

Wait...court? Oh man, this shit just went all the way left. Any who, know your worth, have contracts, keep your receipts, and if need be, take their goofy ass to court!

Angie T:

Yeah... The way it escalated had my head spinning. Like I said before, I'm glad I wasn't at the door because 'court' would've taken on a whole new meaning. I'd already had to transfer money from my savings, so the last thing I needed was to be posting bail!

TRACK 2:
Rich Girl:
Financial and Creative Freedom

NAB:

Allow me to enlighten you on some things that you need to consider if you want to get yo money right. In the entertainment game, especially for us DJs, having both financial and creative freedom is everything. People see us rocking the parties, but there's a lot more going on behind the scenes. A WHOLE LOT! To really make it and keep things fresh, you gotta get your money right and keep your creative juices flowing. I mean if you've never taken classes, seminars, or read books about financial literacy, start last week. Dead ass!

Getting your finances in check is a must. It's not just about making enough to get by; it's about having a stable flow of cash so you can invest in yourself, save for the future, and handle the ups and downs of the business. It's so crucial that money affairs are handled from the get-go so you don't end up taking any type of gig cuz you need the bread. This is how so many people in this industry end up cheating themselves, by doing low paying jobs just because they're broke. Oh, and believe me, I've been there, but I'm a fast learner so I got my shit together real quick.

First off, don't rely only on gigs. The number of shows you get can change a lot. Look into other ways of making money, like producing and selling tracks, giving DJ lessons, or even hosting events. Diversifying your income makes things more stable and broadens your network. I mean personally I leave the hosting gigs for Angie T, but you do you. Basically, everyone in this industry does something else and quite frankly you have to. Especially when you're starting out, you have to be real crafty and keep your options open. There's so many opportunities that can make or break your brand and making sure you do things that are in alignment with your brand is key.

Investing in good gear is super important. Sure, cheap stuff might work for a bit, but quality equipment will keep your sets smooth and professional. Also, put money into marketing, branding, and learning new skills. These investments pay off big time in the long run. You have to invest in yourself if you expect to be taken seriously. Do you have an EPK? A mentor? A business, city, county license? A business bank account (not CashApp)? Insurance? Backup equipment? Bruuuuuhhhh…if you don't have at least those items, then get the molasses outcha ass and get to it!

Budgeting and saving are crucial. Keep track of both your personal and business expenses. Save some of your earnings for the slow months. Having a financial cushion means you can focus more on your music without stressing about cash. Listen… being broke is a distraction that you will pay for in the long run. It's your integrity and worth that will be compromised if you slack on your finances, which will then force you to do any type of gigs for any type of money.

Look into ways to make passive income. This could be from royalties on your tracks, affiliate marketing, or monetizing your presence on platforms like YouTube, TikTok, or Twitch. Passive income gives you financial security and lets you take on projects that might not pay right away but are creatively rewarding. With social media going crazy, like it is making the stupidest people trend, there's no way you can't figure out how to ride that wave.

Stay on top of your financial education. Go to workshops, read up on money management, and maybe even talk to a financial advisor who knows the entertainment biz. Being smart with your money helps you make choices that fit your long-term goals. There's a plethora of information regarding money management available so find whatever tickles your fancy and LEARN. Audible books are my daily source of knowledge but I watch videos and ask questions about money to individuals that are qualified to answer them.

While getting your money right is important, creative freedom is what keeps you passionate and innovative. It means having the freedom to try new things, mix different styles, and create unique experiences for your crowd without being held back by financial stress or market demands. You need to take advantage of all of the opportunities that you are presented with because this industry is full of money. Stay true to your style. It can be tempting to only play crowd-pleasers, but your unique sound is what sets you apart. Make sure to carve out time to produce and play tracks that reflect your artistic vision, even if they're not mainstream hits.

Always learn and experiment. The music scene is constantly changing, so keep exploring new genres and techniques. Taking risks keeps your sets fresh and keeps you excited about your craft.

The F.E.W.:
DJ Kelly J, NotaboiDJ, Angie T

I never would've expected to be on a morning show on a radio station Mon-Fri but I was at the right place at the right time. This platform allows me to reach in my creative bag because it's not a commercial station so I can be pretty much "ME" which is priceless! Sidenote: these are things to consider when choosing to work with commercial vs. public radio. Money vs. freedom. Decisions, Decisions!

Collaboration is so clutch. Work with other artists, DJs, and event hosts. Networking in the industry can open up creative avenues and give you fresh ideas and techniques. When you want to be in this industry, get used to meeting new people and shooting your shot. You never know who's listening and who may be in a position to excel you to newer levels.

Dedicate time to personal projects. These might not bring in immediate cash but offer huge creative satisfaction. Whether it's working on an experimental album, organizing a themed event, starting a podcast, or producing, these projects can reignite your passion and help you grow as an artist. Being diverse is crucial so when you dibble and dabble with various ideas, that increases your worth. Out of everything that I've done in the industry, there's probably more losses than wins but the learning process and connections that were made along the way are priceless.

Engage with your audience. Social media is great for this. Listen to their feedback and let it inspire you, but make sure it aligns with your creative vision. Don't let it control your art. The tricky thing is that people want to be entertained and if you can master that, then that's half the battle. Personable artists are the ones that people flock to and support so do your best to be that, even if you aren't. I'm not big on talking just because I don't have a good filter so I might say something that rubs people the wrong way. Next thing you know, I'm canceled. We're in the era of canceling (ain't nobody got time for that). Less is best so if you really don't have anything to say then don't. TikToks always suffice!

Balance is everything. Make sure you're getting enough rest and personal time. Burnout is real, and keeping a healthy balance between work and life is crucial for staying creative., This is so hard to do while chasing a bag. Especially in Las Vegas where there's always something going on. You keep thinking that you're going to miss out and FOMO will have you all messed up. Sleepless nights, drunk mornings, and tired days will catch up to you, then next thing you know your health will begin to decline. It is not taught or talked about enough in this industry how important balance is, which will be your best friend. We are still human so it's imperative that you take care of yourself. Drink your water, get yo z's, & take a vacation sooner rather than later.

The real magic happens when financial and creative freedom intersect. When your finances are stable, you can take creative risks, and your creative projects can bring in more money. It's a cycle where one feeds into the other, creating growth and innovation.

For example, financial stability can let you invest in top-notch equipment for your gigs, leading to better shows and more recognition. Likewise, creative freedom can make you stand out in the crowded market, attracting more gigs and diverse income streams. Anytime you can, SAVE. This way, you can keep investing in yourself and evolving every time you need to level up. There'll always be more equipment, mentors, conferences, etc., you need to take advantage of.

In the end, achieving financial and creative freedom takes dedication, strategic planning, and a constant drive to innovate. By mastering both, you not only build a sustainable career but also create a legacy that inspires others in the entertainment industry. As DJs and event hosts, embracing this dual freedom transforms your role from just entertainers to true artists and entrepreneurs, shaping the soundscape of the future. Trust me when I say that this is a lot easier said than done and I myself am trying to practice what I preach.

Kelly J:

To keep it 100, I hadn't thought about financial freedom AT ALL when I first started Djing. I was 18, felt in my heart it was what I wanted/needed to do, and have been in that space ever since. Those bills make you think about a lot FAST though! As adulthood came around the corner, the need to consider much more than fun followed right behind it.

I keep coming across the phrase, "Two things can be right." and find more and more scenarios where it fits perfectly. I'm really glad I started as early as I did and had a phase where all I had to worry about was having fun and getting the skill set right. I always had a job, if not 2 or 3, and at the time, djing full time wasn't really a reality yet. There were very few people able to do so and have a decent living. Even fewer with a GOOD living. And so many people looked at it as a hobby. You know, you run into somebody you haven't seen in a while and they ask, "how's your little DJ thing going?" lol. I wish a M.F. would today but, back then it really was a little DJ thing. I didn't know of all the avenues and revenues of being a DJ yet. I was a brand ambassador and model, had another side hustle that deserves its own book one day, and was an up-and-coming DJ, so of course I wanted to be headlining at Drais, like TODAY. Drais was and still is the only all hip-hop club on the Strip in Las Vegas. It's most hip-hop DJs' dream destination. But it's run by agencies that pay pennies, and usually only book celebrity DJs to headline. Unless you're Franny. Franny's another G.O.A.T. And I watched him break every "rule" Vegas tried to throw at him, and he still "made it." But I always wondered if he would've made it at all if he looked like me. It made for a very distorted perception of rules but I came to some sort of conclusion: some rules are there for a reason, and some are meant to be broken. Two things can be true.

I limited my financial and creative freedom in a F.E.W. ways and didn't realize it initially. Pun intended 😁 Mainly because I was having so much fun, I had multiple jobs, took being down for the culture a little too seriously at times, and didn't have the mindset of a business owner... in Vegas.

Everything happens for a reason, and I don't regret any part of my process. I was missing out on huge opportunities though, and both my Detroit roots and my pure Taurus traits weren't having it.

Hip-hop has never come out of the top 4 genres of music since its inception, going toe to toe with rock and country, but still a piece of #1, which is pop. Hip-hop and Las Vegas have the most dramatic, traumatic relationship, and although I know for a fact I wasn't in the first handful of eras trying to figure it out, my era had a LOT to deal with. Locally, I was the only black female that stayed, for a long time. My era may have been the second or maybe even the first era of entertainment in Las Vegas where hip hop was the #1 genre, and the city didn't know what to do, but to better understand this dilemma we gotta go all the way back for a quick history lesson.

Vegas is racist af, the end! Okay jk. Here we go....

A popular synopsis starts with Las Vegas and urban entertainment around the time of the Rat Pack. The three main vocalists, Dean Martin, Frank Sinatra, and Sammy Davis Jr., all have streets named after them in Vegas. Sammy got his last... that's a fact, but man get ready for this story for real, lol. So, the world-renowned, extremely popular, supposed to be respected Rat Pack would get booked to perform in Las Vegas often, and just like today's headlining artists, would get comped hotel rooms at the venues they performed in along with hefty salaries. Not Sammy. Mr. Davis Jr., being part of the Rat Pack, was not allowed to stay in the hotels that he performed in. The 1950s in Las Vegas was still very segregated, and although Sammy Davis Jr. was SAMMY DAVIS JR., he would stay at either the Moulin Rouge while it lasted, or the Harrison House. My connection to the Harrison House is very deep as I've been there multiple times to raise awareness and funds over the years. The Moulin Rouge is long gone.

The Harrison House is a literal home located in the Historic Westside of Las Vegas. The Historic Westside was the part of town designated for the black community during segregated times. In 1942, Genevieve Harrison opened her home to traveling entertainers, business people, and divorcing couples who were unable to stay at Las Vegas strip hotels due to segregation laws.

It's a Historical Monument now, preserved and still standing strong. Sammy Davis, Jr., Harry Belafonte, Pearl Bailey, Louis Armstrong and Joe Lewis are just a few notables that have stayed there.

Although not open long, the Moulin Rouge and the NAACP helped to desegregate the city in 1960. Legally.

Kay so the city is legally desegregated, yay... but Vegas is still doing the most, still coined the "Mississippi of the West" by Black entertainers, annnnnd I'm a black entertainer. Now that y'all have a little history lesson, let's fast forward back to now....

Vegas is STILL racist af but some of the racism is centered around business principles. Yeah, that... just listen. Black ppl spend a LOT in Vegas, but still not more than other ethnicities. And unfortunately if ANY incidents happen, it's used as justification that we can't do sh*t here by the masses. Black people are also a super minority here, meaning we're not the majority, or even the top of the minority population wise, although the culture and music is. So here lies this very thin line of using the music and the culture to attract EVERYBODY, not just black people, to maximize profit now that high-profiting entertainment is centered around it.

This was extremely frustrating and exhausting to learn in my first decade as a DJ. I was never diagnosed with depression but probably treaded the line a handful of times while figuring things out. Then imagine NAB or whomever asking for mentorship?! In my right mind, I would've just said RUN! I had mentors but nobody that looked like me that I could go to that consistently DJed on the strip. I had multiple people that had done fragments of what I wanted to do, but no one person that had done exactly what I wanted to do. The concept of just copying what other DJs did, didn't work which almost left a very bitter black woman in my spirit.

I'll never forget one of the few off days I had where I went to a club downtown with some friends. It was a West Coast hip-hop themed party.

Y'all, no part of West Coast and hip-hop is clean, especially at a party downtown. Certain songs and artists were banned from being played at the clubs on the Strip and downtown. Yeah, in the 2010s. I was so curious to hear what the DJ was going to play knowing that a bunch of songs were banned. Or so I thought. To my surprise, a lot of the songs the DJ played, were the exact same songs in the same sequence that DJs that look like me couldn't play or would get in trouble for playing. I was furious. Like code red, the Bull is out, move tf out the way, right now furious. Why were they able to play the songs, OUR songs, and we couldn't?!

By now, I had just about grown numb to hearing other races say the N-word, especially singing the songs that had the word in it, but the Bull in me saw so much red that night looking around. By now, I knew the city's history. I had my own experiences with racism here and in Detroit. I was losing it in real time, but as I looked around, I saw all races of people singing and/or rapping along while dressed up as 90s rappers. It hit me and thankfully before I hit somebody: ALL races of people were singing and rapping along. It wasn't just black people. This is stupid af, but maybe that's why they were able to play these songs this way. The entertainment capital of the world will seldom turn away a cash cow that's attracting

The F.E.W.:
DJ Kelly J, NotaboiDJ, Angie T

EVERYBODY. I didn't calm down til I had a few drinks, got home and got some sleep, but I understood what I witnessed that night. I had to make some changes.

What I was met with next could've brought out the very cliche angry black woman. I had a lot to be angry about, but I knew it wasn't going to fix anything. It was like "hip-hop DJ" was stamped on my forehead, as many people assumed that was all I could play. Had I played 95% hip-hop most of my career at this point? Uh, does R&b, throwbacks, and Afrobeat count for anything?! I did some digging to study the few black entertainers doing well in Vegas although many of them didn't live here, I saw that they also appealed to everybody, they played some of everything, WELL. They didn't look rich, nor were they flashy. They didn't look like they were a part of any set either. They had a very unique aura about each of them. They knew people and they knew all types of music.

The demand to blend hip-hop in at the clubs on the strip was higher than it's ever been, with pool clubs featuring hip-hop artists dominating the whole year. EDM was still strong, but now featuring hip-hop mashups or even hosted by hip-hop artists. Chile, even the hip-hop artists started Djing. Lounges and clubs off the strip were being created out of the woodwork, but due to the many laws of the Wild Wild West, didn't last long. Vegas had become a hotspot for hosting sporting games, national events, and we finally began to hear talk of major league sports heading here.

My desire to keep the culture alive, establish a stronger brand, have some kinda fun, and stick to root purposes had me all over the place for some years. I wanted to help people feel good and have a good time, and I also wanted to help up and coming artists have a level playing field with getting their music out. But both of these things heavily relied on my brand being big enough to have a voice people would listen to. My brand won't be big enough if I just do hip-hop. The root of this sent me down a rabbit hole of tasks that took years to master in an effort to MAYBE make a difference. To MAYBE be able to influence before being an "influencer" was ever a thing. And of course, earn a good living. But I'm not gonna lie, a large amount of time was spent controlling my ego and redirecting my anger when it came to how Vegas truly operates.

At the turn of the 2020s, hip-hop music shifted, and we started to get what most people call low-vibrational club songs. Songs that talked about shooting somebody, killing somebody, stealing somebody's girl, being depressed, or even committing suicide. AT THE CLUB. The place that was initially for people to escape their problems, had EVERYBODY'S problems front and center. Sometimes literally. I can't tell you how many people got caught up at the club. And nobody was dancing. I hated this sh*t sooooo much.

After dealing with people actually losing their lives at the clubs, being shot at myself, venues being shut down, and now nobody dancing to the songs they were requesting me to play, my love for djing in the hip-hop clubs faded away quickly. Did I mention that the artists I was trying to help weren't even showing up to the places I was playing their music? Chile.

I had Z in 2018 so I really had a new perception of life as a whole; like uhm, I need to get my ass home to my baby after work! And have energy for her. And be happy. So why am I playing all this negative shit? To be popular?! Popular for what?! Is this worth it?

I felt in my heart that I still wanted to be a DJ, but I couldn't play THAT shit. Everyday. Every week. No, no no. So, I started researching things. I went back to that list of popular music and remembered; pop is #1. And pop has hip-hop, but not the depressing, catch a body, be depressed hip-hop. I can do that. In the club scenes, pop clubs are often called open-format clubs, essentially because pop is all of the genres combined. Pop songs are the most popular songs from every genre. I can get jiggy with this! And I did. I started doing more corporate events. Stores, companies, conventions, which led to gigs with Guess, Marciano, Adidas, Amazon, and more. I eventually reached EDM stages and sports teams where I got to experiment with remixes and even remix my own songs. It felt great. I went home feeling good after work again. And now I knew a much wider range of music that reached the entire world. Why TF didn't I do this sooner?! Expanding my creative horizons allowed for the internal peace and financial stability I was yearning for, finally.

To be clear, I'm the hustler. The risk taker. I jump and figure stuff out afterwards. That B word is not my friend at all. I'm talking about BUDGETING. If I need something, I get it before the week is over, somehow. I don't save. Again, having a child changed my entire perception. Although I'm probably nowhere near as financially responsible as NAB, I did change a lot after I had Z. I implemented a lot of things to make sure she and I would always be okay, no matter what happened. And I'm still learning every day. I'll say time and time again that I would DJ til my very last day on this earth, but not full time for sure. Nobody wants to be the 70-year-old DJ in the club, although I did see this new wave of elderly DJs killing it all over the world, lol. I chose a career path that can lead to financial freedom if I structure it properly. And most career paths are the same way.

There's so much being said about the multi-level marketing companies out there. That they're so bad; they're a pyramid scheme; they're a cult; only the top 5% really become wealthy, and on the flip side, how EVERY company in the world is structured like them. Y'all I tried just about all of them. No exaggeration. And I'll tell you this; they teach you the absolute best qualities about mindset. Nobody that actually has financial freedom has gotten there without a ridiculously similar mindset of the people in those MLMs. The only thing different is their focus/target goal.

Your financial freedom starts in your mind. What you think about, speak about. Who you speak to, who you choose to be around. Where and how you spend your time. How you deal with adversity. Your self-discipline. The things you feed your mind. Your consistency.

I told myself I'd DJ full time and be able to sustain the lifestyle I want for Z and I, and I also looked into what that would take. I didn't focus on an exact number, but the lifestyle itself. Every time Z demanded differently from me, I changed my plan. Transparency moment: I had NO clue I was going to be a single mother until I was about 3 months pregnant. My relationship with her father had been bad since the beginning, and after a history of miscarriages, staying in a toxic environment pregnant made no sense to me. So I left and moved in with my mom. Her and I thugged it out til Z was born, healthy, happy, and full of energy. I breastfed Z til she was 2 and a half and that was while DJing full time. When she started potty training, I made a plan and changed my schedule. When she started school, I made a plan and changed my schedule. When she started extracurricular activities, I made a plan and changed my schedule again. When she needs me at home to help with homework or just chill with her, I made a plan and changed my schedule. I didn't just make a wish and wait. Or pray and wait. And these aren't easy plans to make or stick to. The hard stuff just doesn't feel as hard when you're used to doing it, or when you know something great is going to follow it. Manifesting still takes action on your part. Sometimes a LOT of action on your part. Sometimes you have to be in the right place at the right time, letting faith lead you. And sometimes, some sacrifices need to be made. The snowball effect many people speak of is this constantly accruing momentum of small and large tasks, energy, fueling your dreams, goals, and manifestations. Arriving at them is a result of your consistency.

How often were you in the gym? How well did you stick to your savings plan? How often did you pitch yourself to new clients? How much did you practice instead of binge watching tv or playing video games? How much time did you spend researching something you're passionate about? Are you open to learning something new? Have you found a mentor? How do you overcome losses, or adversity? How do you channel anger? Are you still respectful when you're angry? It's all energy.

Angie T:

Ahhhh my favorite part about what I do…The FREEDOM! The freedom to start a line dance out of no-where, the freedom to make everybody put their hands in the air and wave like you just don't care. The freedom to randomly shout: "The roof! The roof! The roof is on fire! We don't need no water let that mf burnnnnnn" I love the freedom to be as bold, black, and unapologetic as I can be. Believe it or not, I'm actually really shy, so 'Angie

T' allows me to step into my alter ego. Being a host has allowed me to host all types of events. I've lead a panel for a Lifetime movie premiere, corporate Gala's, night clubs, and back to school drives. I love that I have the freedom to show my diversity, it's like a form of therapy.

Professionally, there are plenty of freedoms, but also some constraints. Sure, I have the freedom to make my own schedule, but in this line of work, I'm probably working most weekends. Some seasons are crazy busy, while others will have you questioning, 'What was I thinking picking this career path?' I'm free to quit my corporate job and pursue this full time however, there's no packaged retirement, 401K, or health insurance plan to sign up for... Still interested?

I have the flexibility to manage my business as a Professional Event Host while still contributing to my community. I love working with The Cupcake Girls, a nonprofit organization. This nonprofit supports individuals affected by sex trafficking, as well as current sex workers, offering non-judgmental, non-religious-biased help to a well underserved community. The org has an unwavering commitment to empowering voices that might otherwise go unheard.

The F.E.W.:
DJ Kelly J, NotaboiDJ, Angie T

Through this role, I've added Event Coordinator to my list of expertise. Now, when I get booked for events, I can offer coordination as a separate service with real experience to back it up. It's helped me complete the circle of planning, giving me a first-hand understanding of how everything comes together. Truth is, every event benefits from having the host involved before the big day to go over the run of show and make sure all expectations are clear, because the day of the event is too late. Plus, it helps you spot where the client might need extra support or have an idea of your own that can add value to the event. Freedom comes at a price. The more you know, the more valuable you become. So, never be quick to turn your nose up at an opportunity; it just might be the missing piece you need before your big break!

Working isn't a problem for me, as you can see. I be doing too damn much. It's all about loving what you do (or at least liking it most of the time, because let's be honest life be life'ing), being intentional about where you're at and being appreciated while doing it. If what I am spending my time doing daily isn't pouring into me in some capacity, then it's keeping me stagnant. If a job is stunting your growth and keeping you from growing your passion, that's something to seriously reconsider.

As NAB mentioned, Vegas is a lot like NYC and Cali, you've gotta have multiple hustles or streams of income to make it. But in a place like that, discipline is key, because it's easy to lose sight of your main goal while you're busy chasing the bag. For example, is writing this book something important to me? Yes! Is it something I feel God told me it was time to do? Yes! Did I still overfill my plate with additional streams of income for the sake of getting ahead and put the book on the back burner? Sure did! And God slapped me on the back of the neck with his sandal for doing it too. Freedom without discipline can be pure destruction.

I love the freedom to be able to work with a multitude of people and cultures. I'd be remiss if I didn't mention my deep connection & allegiance with the African community. I've hosted festivals, pageants & fashion shows within the African Diaspora. They love and accept my country tail the way that I am! I have been able to learn so much about the culture from being able to work within it. I also had a 1st generation Nigerian roommate (now my lil sis) for about 4 years that was also a life changing experience. Here I am thinking I had to get out of a small-town mindset when baby it's breaking the American mindset that's a whole nother ball game. I want to challenge you, the reader, to try and go to unfamiliar territory! Where does your heart pull you before your mind gives you 17 reasons why you shouldn't? Listen to that! See where you go.

Another freedom I love is being able to bring my people in on gigs with me or we get together and create our own dope event. I'm cut from the cloth of 'if one eats, we all eat!' It hits different when you're actually at the table during the conception of an event idea. In those moments, someone has (and still do) mention my name. As soon as I hear someone needing a service, and I know someone in my camp offers it, I'm putting my people on. But I'd caution you—don't stick your neck out just because you're friends. Their work ethic has to match, or even exceed, yours. Referring someone is like putting an extension of yourself out there, so make sure they're capable of meeting or exceeding the expectation. Otherwise you'll both bear the embarrassment.

Financially, I have the freedom to charge what I want and walk away if we can't reach an agreement. I remember when I started working for a very popular male strip club here in Vegas. I was willing to accept lower pay for the experience and the chance to reach a whole new audience. Plus, I was told I'd make up the pay difference—and then some—in tips, so I wasn't tripping. I was excited for the opportunity to step into the wild side and let my intrusive thoughts take over as host for the night. Let's be real—women are human too, and when a man is fine, sometimes we just can't help where our mind goes. So, I got the chance to say exactly what was on my mind!

I remember coming in on my first night, I was so nervous. Remember, I don't have a lot of experience in the strip club or the male revue area, so I wasn't sure exactly what a male revue host should do. I remember meeting all the guys, they were super cool in their speedos and thongs with boots. Some of them tried to give me the lay of the land and explain how things usually go, which was super helpful. Others, though, gave off serious diva energy and barely acknowledged me. I later figured out that was all a tactic, they didn't want to tip me so they kept a distance. I'll never forget the first day I came to check the club out. One of the dancers pulled me on stage to be a part of his set. Chile, things got crazy! And I mean bananas! (Pun intended 😜) The dance ended with him putting his genitals right on my crown chakra and not in a sexy way! He literally flopped it on top of my lace front and did a wiggle! I was shocked, humored & concerned for my wig! Chile, a mess! I'd later learn that the genital on head bit was a part of his performance and he'd do it to a couple of women each night and they LOVED IT! Outside of that I'm NGL my first night hosting I was a tad bit distracted. Maybe a little turned on... I mean damn muscles, body oil, LED lights and the music going. I tried to not make eye contact cause I didn't want them to see the lust in my eyes. But by the 3rd night working, the infatuation wore off, and I'd see them all as co-workers, so now let's go get this money! I'd ignore some of their diva attitudes or the fact that I've seen the same routine 75 times and just watch the crowd because that's where the money is.

Now the understanding was the additional money was going to come from the tips from customers, so the more excited and entertained they were, the more they would throw some money. Now the tricky thing is, that this particular company prides themselves on not making it mandatory for the dancers to tip out the DJ or Emcee, so I had to basically hope for the best. Needless to say, after going home with $4 in tips twice (which wasn't even enough to pay for my food after I got off work), I went to have a conversation with management to talk about how I wasn't making the amount of money they promised I would. They initially got defensive claiming I hadn't been there long enough, but when I gave them a reminder of the time I had spent there the response was that they'd talk about it and let me know. Less than a week later, I got a text that says my services are no longer needed and they'd mail my last check. Yayy! Freedom!

NAB:

Sidenote…I damn near flatlined when Angie told us she was being paid pennies for penes!!! SMH

Kelly J:

In the realm of the self-managed entertainer, the ups and downs are unavoidable. And it helps to have friends in the industry too, cause we TOLD HER ASS about being over there… smh.

TRACK 3:

Despacito
Dating & Boundaries

NAB:

This is the chapter that I vowed to opt out of cuz I don't like people all in my business, but I was out voted, so here I go. Dating is not for the weak in the entertainment industry. I love men & they love me & they're EVERYWHERE. When I started djing, I decided early on that I wouldn't date industry niggas. Ya know, the type that whistles loud af when they bust. Yall know dude? (OOPS - TMI) For the most part I didn't deal with guys that worked in the entertainment industry, but I kinda did - sometimes shhhhhhh, judge ya mama. It's really tricky trying to get the average working-class man to be comfortable dating someone in this lifestyle. Aside from the fact that he needs to be secure af, he's gotta be flexible, supportive, and understanding. I feel like entertainers/artists are a whole different species.

One time while I was on stage with less than 15 minutes before my gig, I went down a rabbit hole and found out that the guy I was dating had recently bought a house with his alleged ex-wife. A whole house my dude? That shit almost took me out. I think Kelly and/or Angie was with me at the time and had to help calm my nerves. I could feel Fire racing through my veins as I tried to stifle my emotions while doing sound check. I felt like I couldn't breathe, my eyes were getting watery and I was losing my sight. "Calm down, get your shit together, focus, do you know who you are?" These were a few of the lines I told myself to regain my balance after this catastrophic revelation. There was no time to process, confront, pull up or anything. Liiiiiiiiiiike wtf do I do? BREATHE...SLOWLY...IN & OUT...several times. Everything is happening and moving so fast but there's no time to pause or anything.

The show must go on, right? In this industry, we don't get PTO or sick time because nobody really cares about what we're going through. They just want to be entertained. I became fixated on the fact that I had to DJ for just 2 ½ measly hours which seemed like an eternity. I said to myself, "You got this, you don't have a choice, that's what yo ass get for looking, NEVER AGAIN!" Aside from having a nervous breakdown, I was wondering if

The F.E.W.:
DJ Kelly J, NotaboiDJ, Angie T

Kelly would be gracious enough to cover for me. I was literally gonna ask her to do the whole gig for me and let her have ALL of my bread. I needed to go take a drive, cuz you know I saved a screenshot of the address! Whew chile, it's giving... COO COO. Me letting a dude mess up my money? Absolutely the fuck NOT! Those days of letting a man bring out my Chicago ghettoness are over (I think). I sucked it up, did my gig, drank my 2 cups of vodka/soda water w/lime, & got my coins! It was thee longest gig in the history of gigging and it helped me to understand how to perform under extreme pressure. That's when I learned how to NOT look for stuff, argue, or address issues before my gigs. It's imperative that you keep your head in the game and not let your emotions cloud your judgment. Heed my warnings and hold off on any emotional conversations before a gig. What I will say is, the aftermath of that situation was slightly illegal so I will leave the rest up to your imagination. Moving forward in my relationships, my rule is that we only discuss our issues on Sundays because it's safer for everyone that way. Furthermore, I try my best not to go looking for anything that I can't handle if I find it.

With an influx of visitors, long distance dating happens pretty frequently and it definitely had me in a chokehold at one point. Having the chance to travel on a regular basis to get a break from desert living and see other cities is fire...but not being able to have some sausage whenever you want is sacrilegious. Would not advise! On top of that, you spend a ridiculous amount of time on the phone trying to make up for the physical time that you two don't have the ability to spend together. That's a lot of time that takes away from your business and we all know time is money. Day in and day out, I spent anywhere from 5-13 hours on the phone with my long-distance ex-lover & I did this for months (you do the math). TRASH!!! The best thing about long distance relationships is that when they end, at least you don't have to see them again unless they pop up, and sometimes they do (that's another story). Once again, I would NOT advise.

In this industry temptation is plentiful and you can go from meeting in an executive office to smashing beneath a desk in a matter of seconds! And once you cross that line, there's no turning back. I can guarantee you that you will mess up your business relationships and miss out on some great opportunities when you start sleeping with the people that you work with. Las Vegas is indeed a sinful city, with too many clowns that lack morals, self-esteem, & standards. There's a lot of people here with nothing to lose and everything to gain. You never know if someone genuinely likes you or if they see you as their meal ticket. Wisdom & discernment is key and you'll need a ton of it out here in these Las Vegas streets. I still pray for it, daily.

Now let's talk about boundaries. The thing is, if you know who you are, then you won't compromise your integrity for nobody and no amount of money. Rest assured that there's always another dude or gig, and if it's for you then you won't have to smash/suck/lie/snort/coon & buffoon for it. I'm huge on boundaries from the get-go which means contracts are a necessity. The few times that I've done events and there was no written agreement in place, things almost always went left. I can count on one hand how many people still owe me money and in my opinion, that's one hand too many. After I've reached out 3 times to you about my bread, I'm done. Of course, I could seek legal counsel or call the homies to pull up but I prefer to focus my energy on more positive matters. Lucky for them at this point in life, I try to vibrate as high as possible, as often as possible. I have worked too hard and have too much to lose. Ultimately, I'm determined to make better decisions.

I took a gig where I had to bring the full setup to the casino. That means I had to pack my car up with 2 speakers, a table, a dolly, and my backpack. When you work in the casinos that means that you have to walk through a substantial amount of people who half the time are sight-seeing and drunk. I mean, you do the MOST. On top of that once you are done unloading, you have to unpack, setup completely, then walk back through all of the tourists in the casino and move your vehicle cuz most likely you parked in the loading dock, so yup, you gotta move. Anyways, at this point the event coordinator had already given me the deposit but no contract. I Dj'd and put on a party that had the managers at the casino coming in to see who I was. I ran out of business cards that day and had to keep one just to let anyone else take pictures of it. As the event was coming to an end, the event coordinator said that she would give me the remaining balance shortly after she got off of her feet and had some time to relax. I was like, "Cool." Now before you start tripping, I had worked for her before and never had a problem but this time was the last time.

I gave her a few days and then I sent out a text and no response. And then another one…and then another one. Then I started reaching out to others who knew her to see if they could get something from her, and she didn't even respond to them. So, I just had to chalk it up as a loss. A couple hundred dollars that I was gonna have to live without. There's no manual or handbook on how to maneuver through these situations so you just gotta learn as you go. Yes there's the business classes and music classes that you can take at a 2- or 4-year college, but that ain't gonna cut it. Please be a fast learner cuz if not, your ass is grass. When doing business in any field, if someone doesn't want to sign a contract that's a red flag so don't work with them. ON GOD. It's equally important to make sure you're dealing with individuals who have good work ethics.

Most importantly, understanding/protecting your sexuality, along with knowing how to be sexy & still be taken seriously is major. The late hours that I work and all of the equipment that I carry are insane. At any given moment I may have my laptop, 2 speakers, a DJ cascade, a bag with all of my cords, controller and my bookbag.

One ordinary morning before going to the radio station, I noticed that my car was broken into. Thankfully, my equipment was too heavy to carry so it must've been some lazy crackhead, but my smaller bag was stolen. It had my cords and 2 microphones in it, which I needed in a few days for an upcoming event so I had to spend over $700 dollars to replace it. My insurance (hint, hint,

INSURANCE!) only paid for about $350 so that was another loss. From that point on I had to just be absolutely positively sure to lock my car. Fuck that, it was a new truck so I hurried up and went to get the darkest most illegal tent I could afford. I bet you can't steal what you can't see sucker! See how things add up? They don't teach you that in school. The smallest error could cost you thousands of dollars which means that you gotta find another gig to replace the loss, or lock your car, better yet take the items out of your car. Even if you get home and the sun is barely coming up. I've been followed to my car leaving certain venues at no thirty in the morning. All my life I had to fight but I swear I'm not interested in squaring up with all of this pricey equipment on hand.

Fellas...why don't yall offer to walk women to their cars nowadays? Hunh? Being in the limelight gives everyone access to you which is scary. There's been more than a few times that men have popped up to my events expecting to leave with me...like dude are you serious?

With all of the different themed events in Las Vegas, having the proper attire is key. Unfortunately, there's an abundance of women in this city that will wear anything or nothing at all in hopes of attaining success. The thing about this is, that it doesn't usually work out and attracts some of the worst attention. There's a thin line between being sexy & being slutty. Choose wisely! In the vibrant world of DJing, every detail counts—including what you wear.

Pay attention! As you step behind the decks to set the mood and move the crowd, your outfit should reflect both your personal style and practical needs. From the ground up, prioritize comfort and functionality. Choose footwear that provides ample support for those long hours of mixing and dancing. Opt for sneakers or boots that keep you grounded without sacrificing style. When it comes to fabric, breathability is key. Look for materials like cotton or moisture-wicking blends that keep you cool and dry under the spotlight's glare. With the right fabric, you'll stay comfortable and focused on the music. Pockets are a DJ's best friend. Seek out clothing with strategically placed pockets to keep your essentials close at hand.

From USB drives to spare headphones, having quick access to your gear is essential for seamless transitions and uninterrupted sets. Your outfit is your canvas, so don't be afraid to make a statement. Express your unique style through accessories like hats, jewelry, or statement pieces that showcase your personality. Just remember to strike a balance between flair and functionality. Layering is key for versatility. Choose pieces that can easily be added or removed as the temperature fluctuates throughout the night. A stylish jacket or hoodie not only adds visual interest but also keeps you warm during those late-night sessions.

Avoid fashion faux pas that can distract from your performance. Steer clear of overly formal attire that feels out of place in a club or festival setting. Baggy or restrictive clothing can also hinder your movement, so opt for a tailored fit that allows for freedom of expression. Ultimately, your outfit should empower you to command the dance floor with confidence and style. So, whether you're spinning beats in a club, festival, or private event, let your fashion sense shine as brightly as your music. With the right look, you'll be ready to groove your way to DJ success. None of these things are taught in schools but they can make or break your careers so do yourselves a favor and be sure to dress accordingly at ALL times.

When I DJ at the strip clubs you might see me in pasties:

The F.E.W.:
DJ Kelly J, NotaboiDJ, Angie T

And when I spin for conferences, you'll see me in business attire.

No matter what the event is, I make sure I'm dressed accordingly but the most important thing is to carry yourself with respect at all times. This is the best way to ensure that people will take you seriously. And that's all I have to say about that. What you got Angie?

ANGIE:

Whew chill-lay! Don't… No really, just don't! As much as I love my peers, I would never date any of them because I see firsthand what goes down in the clubs and lounges after hours. Besides, I've never been the type to track a man down. Between the late nights, alcohol intake, temptations, accidental hookups, and everything in between wires can easily get crossed. I've lost count of the insecure girlfriends I've encountered. On one hand, I get it sis, the truth is, your man is a Lil'hoe and deep down you know this! HOWEVER, I am not his side hoe! You might want to double-check the chick serving your table or the bouncer giving you a hard time at the door *sips tea*. Yeah… like that! My personal boundary is simple: if we work together, you're automatically off-limits. IDC how 'grown' people claim to be or how discreet they promise it's just not happening!

Majority of my relationships have been long distance which has its pros and cons. It really does take a certain type of confident and supportive person to be able to handle it. We're constantly interacting with folks both behind the scenes and partygoers. There will be some level of engaging or what some would call 'flirting' along the way (in my defense, as a Libra, I sometimes flirt by accident) but I think it's important to really understand the person you choose and trust they have a boundary. I'm stuck between a rock and a hard place because I am over the long-distance thing. I'd much prefer someone who can be present but who is here to date?!! Lol…Truth be told I expect chivalry when it comes to dating. How will I know you like me if you don't write me a letter, send me flowers, and take me out?! It doesn't compute.

I remember a DJ was celebrating his Birthday and both his girlfriends (or at least they thought so) showed up with birthday cake! It. was. WILD! Upon arrival, both women gave their cake to the host to put in the fridge for later so when it was time to bring out the cake, I assume that's when it clicked because both women were demanding their cake back and telling the club owners "You better bring him some lamb chops or something because my cake ain't going." Now I'm coming into this at the very middle of the confrontation, and all I hear is a manager say, "We're bringing out both cakes and that's final." The room was silent and I was like "What?! Oh damn! What now?" They start lighting the candles on the cake then proceed to hand me one. Of course they hand me the cake belonging to the angriest of the two.

So now she's talking to me trying to get the cake out of my hand as I pull it away and balance it with one hand using the other to create space between us. I say, "This is very uncomfortable for me, can you back up some?" She snaps back, "It's MY cake!" and then reaches to stick her finger in it. Now I'm stuck deciding just how far I'm willing to take this for the sake of the cake, because she's clearly not backing down. This could escalate real quick, and the funny thing is, I don't even care that much I just walked into this mess! She made one last attempt to grab the cake, but just as I pulled it away, someone she knew (the DJ's friend) stepped in, got her to back off, and calm down. Mind you, there were about 8-9 people in this office, and not a single person said a thing, just watching. It really goes to show how these men will have you out here making a fool of yourself with zero regard. The birthday boy's only concern was how his 'main chick' (the quiet one) felt, while the one who was the most upset was just left to figure it out on her own. Just tew damn much!

The F.E.W.:
DJ Kelly J, NotaboiDJ, Angie T

Furthermore, I've noticed a lot of the men in and around this industry are straight-up chatty patties, they can't wait to brag about who they've been with. The Libra in me enjoys being the eye candy you look at but can't touch. I'd be lying if I said it was easy because some of them be fineeeeeee as hell, girl! Whew! And sometimes, at 3am after a couple shots of Patron, under the club lights they be looking like a snack BUT it ain't worth it. Besides, my personal preference is a good ole country boi!

I've had a long-distance relationship with a person I thought I'd spend the rest of my life with. We'll call him Mr. Moore. We had been doing the back-and-forth dance since my late teenage years. He was the bad boy I'd do anything for and in his eyes I was 'the one' or Kadijah as he would call me. Over the 12 years span we'd always keep in contact seeing each other when time permits until we finally decided to be for real and do the relationship thing.

I was in Vegas and he was in ATL. We would see each other every month and make the most out of the time we had together. I'd travel back and forth to ATL packing all my recording equipment so that I'd be able to broadcast for the radio show remotely. The pandemic was a very interesting time to say the least, but like 'we' always do' we make it work. Besides, let's be honest, Atlanta was one of the only cities that didn't shut down during the 2020 pandemic. It was business as usual down there. The airport rides back home used to feel like a gut punch. We had a plan to start a life together in Vegas, but as fate would have it, he passed away 3 months before the time came for him to move to Vegas in 2021. Since then, dating for me has been a rollercoaster, but I STILL ain't dating anyone in the industry.

Having boundaries is something that I had to learn to master. I used to let the people-pleasing side of being a Libra govern how much I would allow a person to drag me through the mud. But after a few counseling sessions I learned that, the boundaries (or lack thereof) you set with a person is a direct reflection of how you feel about yourself. And I'm referring to everybody! Sister, mother, boo thang, auntie, boss/job, and best friend. I used to view my willingness to do whatever for the people I love and places that I worked for as a love language, but in the end it was a form of disrespect to self. It is empowering to use the word no, sometimes HELL NO is the only correct answer.

I'll never forget I was working for a company (that shall remain nameless). An employee was critically ill in the hospital for 2 days and before their body was cold the company was already trying to fill the position. I was so shook because this person was a ride or die for the company, and always went above and beyond for them. I'm talking about doing hella work off the clock type shit and more. The fact that they replaced this person so quickly, made it clear to me: in the end, anyone is replaceable. That's why it's up to you to make yourself a priority.

Now when it comes to putting that shit on... Angie T is gonna Put. That. Shit. On!!!! Getting dressed is another form of self-expression and whoever you wanna be & feel that day. Because we set our own schedules, it's tempting to just throw something on and go, but taking an extra minute to dress how you want to present yourself can make a big difference. Sometimes, that small change can kickstart a productive day. Now that you've put effort into your look, you might feel up for attending a networking event you just found out about. Or wearing your favorite business casual outfit could lead to an unexpected lunch with someone you've been wanting to connect with, who you bump into while running errands. When you put a little extra effort into your appearance, the possibilities are endless. I love me a good ole themed occasion! Don't get me wrong

Targé has seen me looking homeless a couple times, but I make sure it's not an all the time kinda thing.

I remember as a kid hearing an old Destiny's Child interview with all 4 members. They said, "We wear nothin' with our butt cheeks out, or our boobs out. We like sexy clothes, but still classy." That has always stuck with me. Don't get me wrong, I'm all for supporting anyone rocking a G-string and a dream. Everyone deserves respect, no matter what. I am here for the girlies that wear a string and a dream outside, I believe you deserve respect either way. Unfortunately, some folks are ignorant and will need to be trained on how to treat you (probably more than once). There could be opportunities missed out on because of it. Is it fair? No, but it's the reality. I'll never say never because if there's one thing social media has taught me is that ANYBODY can become famous. I like to teeter the line but rarely overstep when it's a professional setting, but if the event calls for it then go crazy boo.

At my events I always like to dress the part. Unless it's an outside event or at a venue that requires a lot of walking around, I'll wear heels. I always bring flats or sneakers as an alternative option as well because there's nothing worse than the host of the event walking around like they have thumb tacks in their shoes. I like to go all out so if you say we're doing a Cowgirl theme event then giddy up! I'm showing up with my hat, boots and maybe gloves. Pajama theme party? I'm bringing my pillow, slippers, PJ's, and blanket. Whatever the case you want to make sure you bring your own personal flavor to the theme, people are more receptive to you when you participate in the theme at an event. Besides, it's just fun to do! It makes for great content as well. Here's a pic from me and Kelly J from a Circus Circus themed event:

As the host/emcee you will pretty much be interacting with everyone there, so it's always good to know the lay of the land in order to plan accordingly.

As the host you will be mulled over with a fine-tooth comb by the audience because essentially you are the face and set the vibe of the event so people have to trust what they see. It would be wise to invest in yourself. Start a good skin care routine, work on your resting B**ch face, polish your toenails every now & again, invest in some perfume or a body mist at minimum & keep your hair together. This is another reason why the price is the price because it costs to uphold and maintain such an appearance! Speaking of investing, go on ahead and invest in a portable fan! I don't go anywhere without my neck fan, cause again, no one wants a sweaty ass host trying to greet customers! That Yelp review will not go over well.

Aside from what I have on I always keep my head held high, look people in the eye when I speak to them, and be sincere in my delivery. I'll never forget, the most nervous I've been was hosting NYFW and walking the runway! But I had to keep my head high, my confidence up and SLAY QUEEN.

The F.E.W.:
DJ Kelly J, NotaboiDJ, Angie T

Don't be afraid to tell someone you'll have to think about it and get back to them. I remember I used to always feel rushed to make a decision on the spot, this method gave the Libra in me hella anxiety because 70% of the time I didn't like that option after I had the chance to sit on it. I'm not suggesting to take your precious time but allow yourself a moment to reflect and weigh your options before committing because once you give your word, you are locked in. Don't back track or allow people to try to down talk you when handling business! Trust your gut because at the end of the day we will do good business or no business at all and that's whether I have on sweats or a prom dress. In the end, it won't matter how good you look if you aren't in tune with yourself. This plays a role in how you are viewed. These fast-talking jive turkeys will smell the milk behind your ears and talk you right out of a good deal if you allow them to throw you off your rocker.

KELLY J:

If you're a good-looking woman in any male-dominated field, just about EVERYBODY will try to hit. In entertainment, they'll get really strategic with getting close to you too. Photographers will offer free photoshoots, security guards will go out of their way to treat you like the Queen of England, bartenders will get you wasted for free, managers and promoters will promise you the moon and the stars. Don't get me started on the celebrities. It's better to be the bitch everyone respects than the 304 everybody talks about. Like Ang mentioned, men gossip like crazy nowadays, and honestly I think they're WAY worse than women. You don't want your business in everybody's mouths, it'll follow you everywhere and affect your work. Be in control of the narrative, and a major part of that, is REALLY knowing the person you're dating, which is an FBI investigation in itself....

My dating life has been a HOT MESS since the very beginning. My child's father was also my high school sweetheart, but I was never his, especially since he took someone else to his prom and lied about it… yeah. Fast forward to spinning the block a few times, a couple failed engagements, dating is cool, but I'm tired y'all. I never wanted to be the leader in my relationships, but I won't slow down for anybody nor will I follow anyone off a cliff. Z was a planned baby, but being a single mom wasn't part of the plan at all. I tried making sure I didn't date someone I worked with, and tried dating someone I worked with. It's a hot mess EITHER WAY!

My true Earth element, certain daddy issues and maybe some mommy issues, overall self-esteem issues, mixed with being one of the few females in the local entertainment industry, resulted in failed relationship after failed relationship, after failed relationship. NAB and Angie T are absolutely right, it may not be ideal to date someone you work with. It's extremely difficult to stick to that when: you work EVERYWHERE and you're ALWAYS working, which was the case for me these past 15 years. I dated people I worked with, for a while, I just made sure I didn't mess with the gossipers. Who else was going to understand the payment issues I had with janky promoters? Or the LA and Bay Area music culture overshadowing the Vegas culture? What about us migrating from venue to venue after one is shut down? Or the long meetings and outings where I'm not being paid to be at but it's still work?

Hell, I'm on a stage AWAY from people most of the time that I'm working, you expect me not to talk to the ONLY people that are within physical proximity? The dating pool is horrible in Vegas, and I'm such a sucker for love, but I definitely looked for it in ALL the wrong places!

After a few interventions, I stopped dating people I worked with, which at the time had been a horrible tango with one person that had gone on for some years. We had a big falling out, which would prove to be the first of many in our lifetime. I had just started djing at a few lounges on the Strip and met this fine guy from Florida. We did our thing after the party was over and never stopped talking to each other. I don't do long distance relationships AT ALL. If we can't see each other consistently, we can't be together. I told him that, and next thing I know, we're making plans for ME to move. I got in a full-on relationship with someone who was definitely supposed to be a one night stand AND moved across the country for him! I learned from the many stories among other women later in life that this was truly a thing to do in your early 20s/30s, lol. It worked out for some women and didn't for others. Annnnd, I was in the latter group....

The F.E.W.:
DJ Kelly J, NotaboiDJ, Angie T

DJing isn't the kind of occupation you can easily find work in once you relocate; basically, if you move, you're starting over from scratch with establishing a network to get gigs from. Welp, that's what I did for love (eye roll) ... packed up everything that could fit in my truck at the time, and shipped it from Las Vegas, NV to Jacksonville, Florida. I didn't think about my career at ALL, but it also wasn't as solid as it is now. I didn't have much to lose. But he didn't have anything to lose....

There's a lot of people here with nothing to lose and everything to gain. - **NAB**

I learned then that it's really important to weigh things out COMPLETELY and see all scenarios through. It's a thought process that I carry with me to this very day. At the time, in Jacksonville, Florida, there weren't many female DJs, same as Vegas, so I stood out like a sore thumb. Which was a good thing. I had a network of DJ framily (friends and family) already, and they had helped me get a few consistent gigs and DJ radio slots. Jacksonville is NOTHING like Las Vegas. I had to learn the culture FAST to stay employed. But it was SO much fun! My boyfriend at the time was an OD party goer, which I should've realized was a red flag, but I was soooo "in love" and thought it was dope that he would come to work with me and try to help me get gigs.

You never know if someone genuinely likes you or if they see you as their meal ticket. - **NAB**

Work was just okay; it was nothing like Vegas but to be the new DJ on the block, my name was in all the right places. I think this, and the fact that I literally flew across the country for someone I barely knew, resulted in some immediate issues. At the time, I had 6 years of work backing me up in Vegas, but only a couple of months and the "Vegas DJ" stamp as my ammunition in Jacksonville, and Duval county rocks with their own. I was still a promotional model/brand ambassador at this time, alongside djing, but I hit a rough patch financially, and the boyfriend I was soooo in love with, couldn't hold us down. Couldn't support us or help me feel secure in my decision to move for him. The energy was really bad and I had no family and few friends there.

I started taking promotional model gigs in Georgia and other parts of Florida, and quickly grew to appreciate the drives; the views of tall, rich, green trees along roads that seemed to stretch to the end of the earth, made me want to always be away. It rained a LOT, and my pixie cut hair wasn't having the humidity most days. I noticed him going out of town more often, but I didn't even care. A guy friend from Vegas, the one I mentioned doing the horrible tango with, was working near Orlando, Florida, and I needed to see him BAD. All bullshit aside, we were still friends. I had only been in Jacksonville for maybe 7 months, but that was too long to be completely away from friends and family. I got up early and took the drive from Jacksonville to Orlando to meet up with him. We immediately started talking about work, weather, and all the usual Vegas drama. Super innocent lunch and convo til the very end.

He and I had history; we were never in a relationship but our friendship was never just that either. I told him about my relationship issues and he had just broken up with his longtime girlfriend. It was time for me to get ready to hit the road and head back to Jacksonville, and he asked me something that I never thought I'd hear come out of his mouth. He asked me to leave my boyfriend and come back home to Vegas with him. Not that very second but move back home and actually date finally. I thought I was high, sleep, dead, ALL the things. There was no way this was actually happening! But it was. Everything in my soul wanted to say yes, but I had so many issues trusting him. I could never explain it, but so many times I felt like he was playing with my head. So, what came out was, "No, I can't. I love him." And all the fire in the convo quickly faded. He said, "I will respect it then. "We hugged and said our goodbyes. The drive back to Jacksonville felt like I was driving to Detroit or something. The whole day replayed in my head until I got home.

Man, I was pissed when I got back to Jacksonville. I loved the domestic side of being in a relationship; I was fine cooking and cleaning and all of that, but my boyfriend was starting to feel like anything but that. Not having the financial security, I thought I would have really affected my perception. The convos were becoming cold and felt effortless between us both. Intimacy had just about stopped after a couple weird interactions. Then one convo changed it all: He said, "he loves me but he's not IN love with me." He addressed my short hair, and now my weight had become an issue. Chile... not after I moved for your ass! Not after I chose you over everyone else, especially the ONE guy I'd easily leave anybody for! I had immediately gotten the craziest quick weave I ever had and started working out to try to salvage our relationship, but in conjunction with his newly accustomed wandering eye both in person and on social media, and this lingering financial security issue, my fight was gone; I was ready to go. A family visit to Vegas one Thanksgiving, immediately turned into a permanent move back, and to my surprise, I didn't skip a beat with djing. The guy that I visited in Florida was already dating someone else, but I didn't care. I promised myself I'd do better with my self-worth AND my vetting process, which took a lot of tweaking even after this, lol smh.

Maybe it's something about B-words, but around this time, I began a new encounter with another one: boundaries. I don't think I had any for a lonnnnng time. I've been a genuine people pleaser the majority of my life, and it stems from the fact that I genuinely love people... shrugs. If we're close and you need my right arm, I'd probably give it to you, especially since I'm left-handed. My very much needed concrete wall between self-care and the love for others is something like that wall that a previous president boasted and boasted about building for our country, that was never built. At 30-something years old, I'm still working on the foundation. It isn't that I was never burned because I was a million times. I've been abandoned, hurt, lied to, etc., and still try to see the light in some of these heathens... smh. Some kind of divine intervention always happened when it was time to let go for good though, whether it was a friend literally intervening, which NAB and Angie T actually did for me before, or a random call that completely shifted my schedule, or seeing certain people, my living "guardian angels," having certain dreams, immediate physical changes, or even being stung by a wasp… laawd. Whenever I got to a point where my lack of boundaries was about to f**k up my life, I got a sign. To this day, I always say that my grandmother is my family's guardian angel and has the squad working overtime for all of us. She sends all the troops when I'm about to be at the root of my own demise. When these signs come, I know I only have two choices to choose from: lose everything I worked so hard for, or declare this boundary, loud a.f.

In my opinion, my purpose overshadowed very specific desires, until now. As of late, the signs to uphold boundaries haven't been as extreme, thank God. I'm starting to say "no" a lot easier, especially in instances of moving backwards. Although I cherish my life's story so far, and will always be a giver first, I don't wish to repeat too much of my past.

Evolution is always at the forefront of how I move professionally and personally. If we can't grow together, we can't go together. I did a LOT of work on myself, and I'm still working on things daily. The time of holding somebody down, going through the trenches, that struggle love sh*t, has long passed for me.

When it comes to work, the numbers don't lie. The work I put in from here is from my actual position energetically and spiritually, not from where you think I'm supposed to be. I'm not exactly humble anymore, but I'm not arrogant either. If I f**k up, I'll apologize, mean it, and actually DO better. People emotionally dump on me all the time, so I probably won't tell you anything about me unless you ask. I will treat you with the utmost respect whether you're the janitor or the CEO of a company. Just don't try to play me.

I look at my DJ career like a marathon, not a race; although the finish line is cool, the preparation for it, as well as the journey itself is supposed to be just as invigorating. I think we forget that even a completed marathon can have very distressing moments.

I remember moving back to Vegas from my failed relationship in Florida and getting back into the groove of things. I had an opportunity to DJ at the Hard Rock Cafe on the Strip for a big event, and at this time, I had a point to prove. I'm back, b*tches! I had a good relationship with my previous landlord and she leased a different condo of hers to me. The one I had previously was still being occupied by my god sisters. My ex was trying to get me back, horribly. I had hurried and moved back to Vegas, only to realize that I mismanaged some things. My ex helped me ship my stuff to Florida, but definitely wasn't gonna help me ship everything back. Thank God for my mom. Shipping cars is pricey AF y'all, omg. I put down my security deposit and last month's rent on the condo, got all the bills on, furnished the place, annnnd forgot to pay my car note. Like while I was dealing with my failing relationship in Florida and when I actually got back to Las Vegas. I remember waking up one day to go to the store and my car was gone. I was pissed. I had a black-on-black Land Rover with low miles, clean af, and she was gone. I know the game though, and I was determined to get it back. I knew I had some time to get it back and at a lower price if I caught it at the local car auction. My good friend Joseph and godsister Diana helped me get to and from work most times. Catching the bus with DJ equipment just wasn't an option, and ride share companies were underway, but not officially out in Vegas just yet. My ex was still lingering around via phone, talking about nothing. But we were still talking almost every day.

The F.E.W.:
DJ Kelly J, NotaboiDJ, Angie T

My gig at the Hard Rock Cafe was coming up and I was nervous, as usual. I was starting to feel more uneasy than normal, like nauseous every day. I realized that my menstrual cycle didn't start yet, and usually, big gigs throw it off anyway. But that nausea was real. Come to find out, I was pregnant. Yikes. The timing was a mess, and I had just broken up with my ex. I immediately told him after taking two tests with positive results. We had begun to try to put a plan together, but I still had this big gig on the way and bills.

It was the first time my name was headlined on the Strip. I just wanted to do a damn good job. The person that booked me was someone I worked with before, and the energy was never right with this person. I used to look up to this person so much, but every interaction seemed to get worse and worse. This time around, there was no contract in place, only a verbal agreement, which I despised. But this person was of really high regard out in Vegas, and I didn't really have a choice but to trust his word or not take the gig. He told me that I'd be paid at the end of the night, which was really important because I needed to put money on my rent and prepare to try and get my car from the auction site. The end of the night comes, and I can't find him anywhere. Nobody can. I call and call and text and nothing. I'm pissed. The car auction was in a couple days and rent was right after, I needed my money. And this person didn't care. I learned quickly that a lot of them never do.

After running around the venue trying to find anybody that had seen him last, I gave up and got a ride home. Tears fell from my face as soon as I got through the door of my condo, I guess I blacked out. When I woke up, I was in a pool of blood on my living room floor. It was hard to walk, but I called a cab and went to the hospital nearby. They informed me that I had had an anxiety attack and miscarried. The sharp pain that was already in the pit of my stomach grew even wider, but at the time, I was living alone, with bills due. When they permitted me to leave, I caught another cab back home, and proceeded to find this person, this time with help, to get my money, which I did get, but much later than planned. I lost my car for good. My landlord was really accommodating due to our previous relationship, and had let me pay her late. I started a new relationship with CBD products at the turn of it becoming legal in Nevada to combat my anxiety issues. Losing the baby was an off and on pain that I really had to control, because I couldn't be sad at work, and against doctor's orders, I was still working a lot to try to catch up. I no longer relied on one source of income when I know there's no contract in place, and called people on their bullsh*t early, taking calculated risks. Without ever telling people what happened with my baby, the troops came out locally if I ever said that somebody didn't pay me or owes me money. I also learned then how to write my own contracts and demand that a deposit be paid or turn down a gig with no hesitation.

To pure coincidence, another huge call to action on setting boundaries was influenced by a little one. This time, my daughter Z. I'll never forget getting signed to one of the top DJ agencies in Las Vegas. In Vegas, you have to be signed to an agency to DJ at most of the venues on the strip; the agencies have had those places on lock since the dawn of time it seems! Z was just born and very quickly approaching her first birthday. The agency gave me the longest contract ever, alongside my first gig. It wasn't that great of a gig, and the pay was even more horrible, but when you're newly signed to some of these agencies, you're starting from the bottom of the totem pole in most cases unless you're already deemed a celebrity DJ. I wasn't that yet, so to the bottom I went. Scheduling had become so important, as I had to balance my work schedule with things I had with Z, and bounce that off of the schedule of my mom, my uncle Kym, or my friend, Sharon, who was helping with Z part time. Z's dad had maybe seen her a handful of times by this point but Z wasn't comfortable around him at all since he wasn't around consistently. This juggle with time, and balancing emotions left me exhausted before I'd leave the house most days.

My very first gig with this agency fell on the same day and same time as Z's first baptism. When I began to put the date on my calendar, my stomach fell to the floor. My church at the time wasn't your traditional church, and her baptism required certain people to be present that aren't casually at the church, so there was no rescheduling it. I called the owner of the agency to let him know of my dilemma, and you would've thought I said f**k that agency, literally. His tone, which was already cold, became even colder, and he said that if I didn't make the gig, that I'd be dropped from the agency. I knew some of the other DJs on the agency's roster, and asked if someone could cover for me. One of the DJs offered to help me out, so I called the agency owner again. Same cold answer: if I didn't make the gig, I'd be dropped from the agency. I'll never forget the pain I felt that day. There was no other option for me to make really; I let him know that I wouldn't be there, and that I hope to be reconsidered with the agency in the future.

The F.E.W.:
DJ Kelly J, NotaboiDJ, Angie T

I don't play when it comes to my daughter. With anybody. This was an important personal matter that influenced a career decision, but I am a mother first. It felt like I threw my DJ career away because now I'd be completely on the outside of the strip again, looking in. But the very next day after Z's baptism, I received a phone call that reinforced my decision to do what's best for Z and I first. The call was from a different agency, booking activations for Nike. They didn't book me for one, or two, but three activations with Nike over the summer, one of them being their 25th anniversary in Florida. Not I got flewed out!!! A new avenue of gigs was introduced to me and although I was still upset about not being with the first agency, this opportunity definitely made up for it! I don't know what would've happened if I didn't choose my family's priorities first.

Sex still sells, even though social media has pretty much numbed us all...laawd. If you're attractive, and in a position to use "what you got to get what you want" (y'all this line from Player's Club lives rent-free in my mind), have at it. But know WHEN to turn it off. Like NAB said, being sexy at a family festival or political event probably isn't a good idea, and if you do a wide range of events, your followers will represent that, so you may tread a different line on how you present yourself on social media from another person in your field that may only do nightclubs or strip clubs, for example. Your BRAND becomes part of your resume, and sex appeal takes on multiple levels.

My levels changed over the years as I allowed my brand to reflect the actual evolution I felt professionally and personally. I started djing and modeling in 2008. It was the tail end of the urban modeling era; the time before social media where medium height, curvy models could get paid modeling jobs. Paid music video features, photoshoots, magazine features, and in Vegas, really high paying gigs at the conventions and after parties. It came and left so fast... with the emergence of social media. There was a drug that is still taking over the masses today; the desperate need for likes and followers. Models were posting their exclusive images before releases, posting explicit photos for likes and followers, and messed it up for everybody. We watched budgets get smaller and smaller, until the infamous "for exposure" tag developed. I don't think I'll ever forgive social media for taking that away... any who.

From 18-23 ish I was mainly in the clubs and industry events and wanted to be seen while perfecting my craft...until a scandal emerged that started to interfere with my gigs. More on that in another book maybe. From 24-26, I calmed down quite a bit and started to dress either more casual or more professional with very little edge. I've been curvy all my life, and doing a little bit came off as a lot to somebody, every time. To be honest, I was irritated and a little bit scared due to the scandal. I didn't want too much attention. And around this time, people were extremely vocal with expressing their opinions about damn near anything I posted or said. I'd get messages saying something was too raunchy, or something I said had offended them. Friends, affiliates, and associates had their kids following my pages, and now there was more pressure to be a better example. People were getting on my LAST nerves for opinions I never asked for, but I WANTED to be a better example.

On top of that, I was floating through the radio stations, with a few big gigs here and there, and a desire to make it to the next level, whatever that meant. At 27, I hit a sharp turn when I became pregnant with Z. I hid my pregnancy until I was about 6 months, changing the style of my photoshoots so only my face or part of my body was shown, posting flyers with older photos, wearing really big shirts and loose dresses. I was so unsure if my pregnancy being announced would stop my gigs altogether. I was again receiving the opinions of multiple people, both in the industry and out, of what I should expect. To my surprise though, I was embraced and supported fully. Like FULLY.

My club gigs were accommodating, everybody and every restaurant was bringing me food, and I had interns to help me with gigs. My gigs didn't slow down until I had to; Z was high risk and I had to get a cerclage. I was put on "bedrest" but was still djing, now seated, about twice a week, every week. After she was safely born, I hit the ground running. Maybe faster than I should have. She was born on a Wednesday afternoon, and I was back in the club djing that following Saturday. A couple of things there, lol. There's no maternity leave for DJs, I was a single mother to a newborn AND djing in what's probably the most competitive market in the world. I got back in the gym, and alongside breastfeeding Z, my mommy weight was going in the right places. I was in better shape than ever before, and now had a much longer resume and larger motivating energy behind me. My branding completely changed here; I had found a new aura that worked for me both as a professional DJ and a mom. It's a level that I haven't really changed leading up to now. A popular model often mentions being sexy with your eyes, smizing, and that's what I'm on, fully covered if I'm ever unsure what level I'm supposed to be on. Nobody is getting in trouble for sexy eyes, lol. That, skill, and confidence goes a long way.

BARS & BEATS

TRACK 4:
Brighter Days
The Power of Community

NAB:

Whether you're spinnin' tracks as a DJ, hostin' the livest events, or just tryin' to make a name for yourself, it's all about community engagement and giving back. Let's break it down without all the fancy talk and have some fun while we at it!

First off, let's chat about why community engagement is the heartbeat of any successful entertainment career. Picture this: you're at a party, spinnin records,' and everyone's vibin.' Who's making it happen? You and your crew, that's who. But it's not just about the bars and beats; it's about the people who support you, show up for you, and spread the word about your talent. When you engage with your community, you're building a loyal fan base. These are the folks who'll show up rain or shine, who'll repost your latest mix, and who'll scream your name from the rooftops.

But it ain't just about getting love; it's about givin' it back too. So, how do you do that?

DJ Kelly J and Angie T are most definitely my crew and it all started out at 88.1 radio station. I never thought that I would have that opportunity, but it's hands down the most rewarding place to ever work at. There's a multitude of ways to become involved with the people and give back by working at a community radio station. Through them, I've been privileged enough to perform at the annual Martin Luther King Jr. Day parade, host food drives, DJ the annual Juneteenth and Jazz festivals, work with schools, teach DJ classes for kids summer camps, and too much more to mention.

Nothing compares to the satisfaction I get when being engaged with the community and they finally can put a face to the name that they hear every morning blasting through their radio. "NotaboiDJ? Is that you? You don't look nothing like you sound! Girl that was so funny when you said that! Or…what you said was so important, thank you!" One thing's for sure and two things for certain, I'm not at all sensitive but in these moments that allow me to connect with people and hear their feedback definitely tugs on my heartstrings.

The F.E.W.:
DJ Kelly J, NotaboiDJ, Angie T

Another thing that I adore is teaching and mentoring. Being someone that individuals, especially kids can look up to in order to see another way of thriving and becoming successful is magical. The fact that I can teach people the things that I had to learn the hard way and wish that someone would've taught me is huge!

In this male dominated industry, it is filled to capacity with dudes who have low self-esteem and ego issues that don't want to help anyone get ahead. Honestly, from my observation these are usually the mfs that's still struggling and looking at people like "The F.E.W." all frowned up and shit wondering how we made it. Yall wanna know how? Do you? Are you gonna listen? Ok, well listen to this…WE GIVE BACK!!! It's really a no brainer, and quite disgusting to see how selfish people are out here in these streets. At the end of the day, you get what you give. I love helping people, especially because I wouldn't be where I am today if people weren't gracious enough to help me.

Now, let's get real about why giving back is so important. Sure, it's great for your rep, but more importantly, it's the right thing to do. The entertainment industry can be cutthroat, but it doesn't have to be. By giving back, you're creating a positive ripple effect that can change lives. It really takes a special kinda stupid mf to not want to give back and believe you me I see those folks all too often out here. I stay far away from selfish people who are only concerned about their own growth and personal gain from every situation. We all tryna eat but working with and for the community will pay off in the long run. Besides, we all need help sometimes, so just remember you reap what you sow. Sidenote…this doesn't give big businesses & billion dollar franchises the green light to take advantage of your giving spirit.

During one summer, I was afforded the chance to volunteer at a kids summer camp and another thing I've come to realize is that summer (outdoor) gigs (in Las Vegas) are not for NotaboiDJ. Arriving at gigs early is standard but sometimes it still doesn't allow you enough time to take corrective action. Picture this…I'm taking my sweet little time unloading ALL of my equipment because honestly it's way too hot to do anything at a fast pace. Next, I set up my controller, plugged in all of my cables to the speakers, introduced myself and spoke to everyone who wanted to know who the female DJ was that was about to turn up. Finally, I pull out my laptop for the last piece to complete my layout and BOOM…it wouldn't turn on. Whhhaaatttttt??? I was certain that it wasn't dead but I plugged it up and waited a while to see if it needed some juice but nope. Suddenly, it dawned on me how hot the bottom of it was and I realized that it had overheated in that short timeframe. Mannnnnnn…all I could tell the coordinator was to give me some ice (lots of it). By this time, the event had already begun and every now and then, someone would casually look over in my direction to see why I hadn't started my set. The ice arrived and I had a towel in my car that I wrapped the ice in, then proceeded to wipe my computer down. Did I mention I was praying? It was like 108 degrees and at that point I knew it would be my last gig outside during the summers of Las goddamn Vegas. About an hour into my set, it finally powered on and I was able to start DJing. On top of that, there were artists scheduled to perform and I had their music on my laptop. Some of them performed acapella cuz we know the show must go on, and that it did. It was giving "embarrassed" to the tenth degree and I apologized as much as I could to everyone who would listen. All the while I was sweating from the intense temperature, it was just racing down every crack and crevice of my body. YUCK. I hate sweating. Let me say this loud and clear to everybody listening, "Please don't ask me to DJ outside in the summer in Las Vegas." Spread the word.

It's important to find a cause that speaks to you and get involved. Whether it's playing at a fundraiser, donating a portion of your earnings, or volunteering your time, every bit helps. Support local programs that provide opportunities for underprivileged kids and teens. Music along with entertainment as a whole can be a lifeline for those who need it most. And don't be afraid to use your platform to speak out on issues that matter. Whether it's social justice, mental health, or education, your voice can make a difference. We're in very powerful positions to influence the world on various levels so we have to be mindful of what we're playing and what we're saying. One reason I don't care for talking is because I don't have a typical "group thought" type of mentality and I know that a lot of my views are controversial so keeping them to myself is fine with me. Also, there are certain artists that I just won't play no matter what due to the negative impact it will make on our community. If you listen to me enough you'll figure it out, cuz with me you gon get this culture. PERIOD!!!

One year while DJing the MLK Day parade with 88.1, it was all type of stuff going on. Parades come with a set of challenges already due to the fact that you are standing on the back of a truck while it's driving and you're trying to spin, plus keep your equipment from flying off of the truck. The weather is usually nice but the sun don't be playing, good thing I had a tent to provide me with some refuge but man oh man, that didn't stop the rain. Aside from the minor whiplash I probably had from the constant stop and go of the truck, a storm was coming. Sweet baby Jesus, on that day all I could do was pray that we'd make it to the finish line before it started to pour. Tent or not, NO equipment is waterproof and who the hell wants to take that risk anyways. We slowly made our way through the line in the nick of time before it started pouring. As soon as the truck stopped for me to start breaking down, it started drizzling and all I could do was hall ass. I was in a pickup truck and they still had to drive me and my equipment to my car. Using my tablecloth to cover up everything while the driver flew through downtown Las Vegas traffic in the rain to get me to my car seemed like a blur. Whew Chile…that was a close one. Thank you God.

To sum it all up, community engagement and giving back aren't just nice-to-haves; they're essentials for anyone looking to make it big and stay real in the entertainment industry. Remember, it's about more than just the fame and fortune; it's about the people who got you there and the ones who'll keep you going.

High key, the community will make or break you because word travels like wildfire. All it takes is for you to be an asshole to the wrong person and next thing you know they'll have your whole character assassinated all over social media. Please don't act like you don't know that this is cancel culture, which means your ass will be grass in a heartbeat. It's simple: being humble, moving with integrity, and remembering that everyone started from somewhere will help you massively in this industry!!!

ANGIE T:

This is IMPORTANT! THE PEOPLE are all we truly have. When I arrived in Las Vegas in June 2016, I was determined to connect with the community here, just like I had back home in Louisville, KY. I wasn't new to networking and community engagement, I'd already learned how to confidently attend events solo and use my Libra charm to make new friends. Networking events are where small talk thrives! You might start the same conversation with a bunch of different people but stick with it! The conversation could go in all kinds of directions, or maybe nowhere at all, and that's okay. The only thing I'd change would be to approach networking with a bit more intention, by doing research on who was going to be there, what they do for a living, and why we need to connect, at the very least. Back then, I was just popping up at events after seeing a flier, with no real idea of who I wanted to meet. I was just there, lol. Don't get me wrong, it worked out, but it's a lot more effective when you show up with even a small plan in mind.

Upon my arrival, I joined my first internet radio show. I loved the freedom of speech and I appreciated my internet radio family. At this point internet radio had just really started becoming a thing, so not a lot of people were hip to the format. Nonetheless, I was pushing my product like it was the hottest show in the world, Craig!! I'd meet all types of interesting people from performers, political advocates, musical artists, and makeup artists. I even think one time I had a jeweler that specialized in watches on my show. We would be in the studio cutting up! This is how radio became my first love. I love being able to connect and have a meaningful conversation with people from all walks of life. I'm not big on fluff. I want you to tell me about the hardest time of your life and how you got through it all, in detail! Not everybody needs to go through it to learn from it. Some of us will take your word for it and change their plan.

I kept engaging with the Las Vegas community, networking like crazy, and before long, I was asked by E. Class Ent to host my first red carpet gig for a fundraiser. It was a male auction where women could bid on men, for a chance to go out on a date and the funds going back to the community (gotta love Vegas!). Opportunities like that helped me gain experience and get my feet wet on the carpet. To this day, I still have so much respect for E. Class Ent for taking a chance on me when they didn't have to. It was there I met the infamous DJ Certified (God rest his soul).

Me and Certified grew closer, and I asked him to help me get on at the local radio station in Vegas. Without hesitation, he helped me put together an air check to submit with my application. After some serious follow-up, I got on the station! For the most part, I was received with open arms and I was happy to be there. There were a couple comments of "Who is Angie T?" "Where did she come from" and "You're ok but not like that" blah blah blah. Doesn't matter, I was there because I deserved to be! I learned quickly how to tune out people's words and get to work. Because you will choke on each letter by the time I'm done.

This particular station coined themselves to be 'The People's Station' and a training station. Both are true. It was a public radio station so we'd have everyone from political leaders to music artists stop in for an interview. I'm still geeked that I was able to interview Kamala Harris when she was running for VP and Spike Lee!!! At any given time, we could have several different community events in one weekend! We'd promote it on air, do a live remote at the location, host the event or interview the organizers about it. Election season was like the Olympics for us because at any given moment it could be an all-hands-on deck situation and literally every employee would be spread out all over the city in an attempt to be at 5 different events at the same time. I learned how to run a board, produce a show, edit talk breaks, record voice overs for commercials, and most importantly emcee a crowd.

The station had an event every Friday night and people from all ages between 21-88 would be there and the DJ & emcee would be live on radio for 5 hours, so you had to come with it! My favorite host to watch starting out was Simply T hands down. Coming into the FM radio world from internet radio, there were a lot of things to learn and tweak. I appreciate him for taking the time to teach me and not feel threatened by my presence & light. He gave me pointers on how to have better talk breaks and during the Friday night gigs, he motivated me and helped me maintain my energy throughout the night. He taught me how to be a dope ass consistent host for an entire event.

I've realized that, much like any other skill, hosting is a muscle you have to work over and over again. Pushing through those awkward moments or the nights when you didn't perform your best is key. You've got to remember there will always be a next time, and when that time comes, you step up with more confidence and try again. Take note of what you think you could've done differently and get feedback from a few folks too, because sometimes, we're just too hard on ourselves.

I used to get offended when the crowd wasn't immediately vibing with me or interacting the way I wanted. In my head, I'd think, 'Forget y'all then, with ya lame asses!' Shameful, I know, but I'm not lying, lol. I realized that mindset was ego-driven and almost a defense mechanism. People won't always react the way you want right away. It doesn't mean they don't like you or aren't having a good time.

This thinking was always debunked by the end of the night, when partygoers would come up to me saying how much fun they had, how they enjoyed my emceeing, and even asking about my other events. How about that?! Here I was thinking

The F.E.W.:
DJ Kelly J, NotaboiDJ, Angie T

I was bombing, but people were actually having the time of their lives. I still laugh about it because it's wild how insecurities and self-doubt creep in. How did that even get planted in my head in the first place?

I worked on air on the Morning Show through the pandemic, which was bananas. We were showing up to the station sanitizing everything trying to stay a safe distance from each other while keeping the energy of the show we had built. Before long, we were recording remotely and trying to hold on to our sanity at the same time. A group of 5 turned into 2 me and Tanisha, and it was quite the task to produce, record and edit talk breaks for a 3-hr show 5 days a week for a stipend every 2 weeks. It was all passion at that point. Clearly, we LOVED radio and the community that we served. We knew the importance it served to the essential workers who would tune into us each morning and even the people who watched us on FB live. We'd get DM's and comments all the time voicing their appreciation for us keeping it going. For some that's all there was to look forward to I mean we were "shut down." Well… everybody but the good folks down in ATL, lol.

Tanisha is another radio rockstar! Her voice is golden, she's super witty and such a team player.

I've learned so much from watching her on air and on the back end of the radio.

Once things started clearing up outside, it wasn't so calm inside, and it was time for me to step into my next chapter. This was a tough learning curve because it was a hard decision. I loved what I was doing and the people I was serving, so walking away felt like I was leaving both the people and my career behind. But for my mental health, it had to be done. To my surprise, the community came through and uplifted me. Many didn't ask why I left the station or what happened; they just encouraged me to keep going and offered support in whatever way I needed. That was the warm hug I didn't know I needed! A reminder that I was Angie T before and will continue to be Angie T after.

It's important to recognize how we place value on the spaces we experience. Staying comfortable can suffocate a dream just as quickly as not chasing it. While routines are great, we have to remember that growth requires change. After being in the same space for so long, we stop challenging ourselves to see what's beyond the wall, and we stay, even when things start to make us uncomfortable or push us to leave. But somehow, we convince ourselves we should stick it out. Let me tell you though, God will keep making it uncomfortable until you finally get the message.

I remember I used to always see Kelly J djing at all of the community events, like literally all of them. I would be inspired by her grind and work ethic, like the girl's got it! As a matter of fact, Kelly J was a guest on my internet radio show! Those were the days.

My favorite type of community event to host hands-down would be anything with kids. Back-to-school, Halloween festival or a pep rally, I am here for it. I remember doing a back-to-school event, and just a couple weeks before, I fractured my ankle. I was so disappointed. By the time the event came around, I had a crutches & a boot on my foot, which thankfully took most of the pressure off of my ankle. So, I was good enough to show up and make it happen. *Disclaimer* I am in no way suggesting that you wobble your fractured ankle down to any event and host. I am simply telling my story lol. But I told them I'd still be able to make it, as long as I can sit down and wear my boot with my crutches, we're fine.

We had the best time at this event! That's what I love most about kids, you don't have to have a lot. You don't have to be anything specific. Just be authentically you and they can feel that. We were doing the Stanky leg, the Nae-nae and all that! They didn't care about my foot being in a boot. As a matter of fact, we played a game of limbo with my crutches! Yes you read that right, I had another kid hold my crutch on the other side and we had a limbo contest. The kids just wanted to have a good time and that's what we did. Needless to say, I had to prop my foot up for a day or so afterwards to get the inflammation back down but it was worth it. I have connected with a couple families from events like this and I keep in contact to this day. Sometimes I'll go up to their school and read to the class or assist with whatever I can help them with. #Community

I recently found a new passion, bringing together inspiring Hosts and MCs from the area to share experiences. As I started doing more events, people reached out for advice, and I kept answering the same questions. That's when I thought, 'Why not get everyone in a room and let's talk about it?' The meetings have been impactful, and the feedback I get afterward shows I'm on the right path. I've built a community where we can discuss the industry and support each other. I think it's important to have, it's a first of its kind here in Vegas.

The F.E.W.:
DJ Kelly J, NotaboiDJ, Angie T

Kelly J:

The Las Vegas community could DEFINITELY have my right arm if they needed it. This city has shown me love in ways I could never have imagined, and I wasn't born here. It would only be fitting for me to extend myself whenever I can to give back. Still working on the "whenever I can" vs. "whenever people ask me," lol. For the last 15 years to this day, the majority of my clients have been word-of-mouth referrals, mainly in Las Vegas. From private parties, to weddings, to radio stations, to billion-dollar corporations, to tv shows, all mainly referrals. Sometimes I still don't believe how much support I get, and often feel like I need to do so much more.

These two concepts molded my idea of a DJ career; the idea to help people via music and an addiction to the advancement of the Las Vegas music culture. Both of those concepts kept me heavily involved in the community even when my brand expanded to other genres and avenues. From the radio stations I worked for, to the community leaders I built relationships with, to the many protests around town surrounding national tragedies of injustice, to kids events. Even before Z, I loved djing for the city's children. A lot of these were done for free, and some are still done for free. Although stretching myself completely thin is never the goal, there's simply a lot of work to do in the community. If I get a call, and I'm available, I'm there.

I'm an entirely different person now on social media than in the years prior, but I very vividly remember being fed T.F. up with the entertainment scene and wanting to quit, to the point where I posted that I was going to quit DJing. People FLOODED my phone, texts, notifications, and private messages either telling me not to quit, how I motivated them or someone they know, or what I mean for the community. So, after a couple times, I shut up and pushed through whatever I was going through. My post and delete game was intense for a while, lol. But over time, I realized that the challenges are inevitable AND not everything needs to be broadcasted on social media.

I had an intern when I was pregnant with Z, Jazlyn Rich, who very quickly emerged on the scene as Vegas' most sought-after female DJ. One evening when the Vegas winter actually felt like winter, she asked to rent my speakers for her event downtown. While I was setting up the equipment, someone went into my car and stole my DJ backpack, with my wallet, laptop, headphones, and external hard drive inside. I wasn't gone longer than 3 or 4 minutes and knew someone was watching my car. I thought that was it! This is where my career ends. I didn't care too much about my wallet; this was right after COVID and I had the access to apps to quickly deactivate cards. But yo, they took my laptop and my external! I had well over 300,000 songs on that external. Work was going well, and I had two gigs later that week. What am I going to do?!

I had an iPhone and my laptop was a MacBook so I immediately went to Find My Mac. I saw that my laptop was still in the neighborhood. I called a few friends, one of them being my homegirl Trenia from Detroit and DJ So Hype. Trenia came quick af, like I don't know if she was already in the area or something but it was like a bat signal went out and she came. So Hype said he'd come after he got off work. Some of Jazlyn's friends helped me look for clues nearby. Someone found the components of my purse emptied near a trash can on the corner. According to Find My Mac, the laptop was a few blocks away. We all went searching for it.

There was a displaced man nearby that told me to go to an area and ask for a man in a cowboy hat; that he knew where my bag was. By this time, So Hype showed up; he had just finished one of his gigs and came straight there. I told him what the displaced man told me, and we drove our cars to an area hidden near the train tracks behind the fence of a popular warehouse downtown. There were about 4 or 5 people back there, all displaced, scattered. Their belongings were in piles that I guess sized their personal space back there. One guy had made a fire in the middle of the area to keep everybody warm. It was late, and everybody was getting cold. Including my damn near anemic self. So Hype was arguing with everybody as I sat next to the fire, I didn't care. He threatened this one guy to tell us where the man with the cowboy hat was, and the guy said he'd only tell us if So Hype bought them some food. And sure enough, he went to Jack in the Box to buy them some food. I stayed with So Hype's friend and some of the people that were living back there. We began chatting, and one man mentioned that I might know his daughter. He showed me a picture of her, and I did know her. I saw her a few times at events around town. He mentioned how he came to Vegas from Cali after trying to get his acting career going, but unsuccessfully, and fell on hard times. Some of the other people back there opened up as well, telling me how they wound up back there.

When So Hype got back he was irritated as hell, but I was just glad he was there. By this time, the guy with the cowboy hat came from behind another fence, and he had my purse. My purse was inside my DJ backpack. I told So Hype he has my bag because my purse was in my bag. The man in the cowboy hat was trying to finesse I'm sure, so he teased the idea of him having my backpack or not, as if he'd only give it to me if we gave him more food or money. So Hype lost it and was about to fight the guy. I never saw his hood side come out til that night, lol. He grabbed him by the collar and told him to come up with the bag A.S.A.P. The man in the cowboy hat gave in, and walked back to the fence, this time unlocking a box. He came back with my backpack!

Somebody went through ALL of my shit; I felt so violated. My headphones were gone, my laptop was gone. But my external hard drive was still there! I had done an okay job of backing up my music and had everything except the last few months of new songs on my external. I was so relieved. I showed So Hype and told him that my laptop wasn't in there. He approached the man in the cowboy hat again, as if to hit him, and the man stumbled and uttered that there wasn't a laptop in the bag when he found it. He mentioned that he found it near a trash can, and it sounded like the area where someone found components of my bag earlier. When I last pinged the laptop on Find My Mac, it wasn't in the area we were in either. I believed him. I told So Hype to leave him alone, and we left.

I got home and told my mom and to this day I still don't know if she believes me. Thinking back, I'm still like, "Did this shit really happen?!" But it did.

I made a post about it, and it's safe to say the news went viral. The next day, my phone had gone off nonstop to confirm what happened and to see if I was okay. My very good friend, AK, made a post on her own, asking the community to help me by chipping in whatever they could for a replacement laptop. I'm sure she knew I was too proud to ask for help in that way. But in a little over a couple of hours, AK calls me and asks me if $700 is enough to get a replacement laptop. She said money was still coming in too. I asked her to stop; to tell them I have enough and not to accept any more donations. She couldn't believe what I was saying. But I was so serious. I knew I could get a really good laptop, better than I originally had, for about $700. And I cried for about an hour after that because I REALLY did need help and couldn't believe that the city had my back like that. She posted that I had enough for a laptop, and she and I thanked the city publicly. The city could have my right arm, but AK could have my left arm. I could never repay her or the community for that kind of support, but I always try my best.

Later that day, I bought my laptop and began to transfer my music and prepare for my gigs for the week. I also bought some snacks, socks, hats, and gloves with the leftover money that the city gave me for my laptop. I went back to the area behind the fence of the popular warehouse and left the bag of items near the fireplace where I sat with the people the night before.

NAB:

WTF? You went back? This that DJ Kelly J shit bruh. They should've stole yo damn car! Only Kelly!

Angie T:
Whew Kelly J bless your heart...

Kelly J:
Whatever man lol....

BARS & BEATS

TRACK 5:
Eye of the Tiger
Anchored Ambition

NAB:

I n this wild world of entertainment, it's easy to lose yourself or become yesterday's news. Whether you're behind the decks, holding the mic, or hyping up the crowd, staying ahead of the curve and avoiding stagnation is crucial. Let's chop it up about keeping it 100 in this ever changing scene.

First off, never forget where you came from. Your roots are what make you unique. If you're a DJ who grew up spinning vinyl in your mom's basement, don't lose that flavor even when you're rocking a crowd of thousands. If you started freestyling in the schoolyard, let that raw energy shine through. But don't be afraid to evolve. Add new elements to your style. Experiment with new sounds, techniques, and ways to engage your audience. Always remember that your squad is crucial. Keep people around who challenge you, support you, and keep you grounded. Your homie, your mama, Bae, your friends, family, your host should all have your back and keep you in check.

Stay away from yes-men and energy vampires. You know the type: they suck the life out of you and leave you feeling drained. Ain't nobody got time for that. I've seen too many talented folks get caught up with the wrong crowd. They start surrounding themselves with people who only care about the limelight and not the craft. Although sometimes it be your own people. Those energy vampires can drain your creativity and enthusiasm. Keep a tight circle of real ones who have your best interests at heart. Remember, "You're the average of the five people you spend the most time with!" My crew has been with me through thick and thin, and their support has been invaluable. We disagree quite often but for some odd reason we just work. On some things!

The entertainment industry is a grind. Late nights, early mornings, endless gigs, it can wear you down. But it's important to find a balance. Take care of your mental and physical health. Meditate, work out, eat right. And remember to take breaks. Go on a vacation. Chill with your family. Life's too short to be burnt out all the time. Trust me, it's so easy to become exhausted in this high-paced industry, it's just so fast and changes so often. When spinning at one of my regular gigs, I was nauseous af and kept running to the bathroom. Thankfully, the closing DJ had come in early and finished the gig for me because I had to take my sick ass home. I legit was so sick that I had to call my lover at the time for a ride due to not being able to drive. All night I barfed and was sick for a few days. I never really knew what was wrong (No I wasn't pregnant). This was one of the scariest gigs for me cuz the show must go on and if I didn't have someone there to fill in for me idk wtf I would've done. I'm grateful for guardian angels! This really was another reminder that it was imperative for me to slow down. Be wise and take care of yourself!

I can't stress enough how important self-care is. There was a time when I was doing back-to-back gigs, working a full-time job, waking up early, going to sleep late, being a mother, and having a tea business. I was running on fumes, and it showed in my health. It wasn't until I took a step back, focused on myself, and recharged my batteries that I realized the importance of balance. Now, I make it a point to take regular breaks and prioritize my well-being. I'm a quite spiritual person and was losing the discipline that I had been used to which was taking its toll. That'll do it! Now religiously, I'm up every morning spending time stretching and praying so that I can start my day with a sound mind, body, and spirit. Oh, plus consuming water & fruit first thing in the morning is the breakfast of champions!

The moment you think you've made it, you're in trouble. Always be hungry for more. More knowledge, more skills, more experiences. Stay curious about new music trends, new tech, and new ways to connect with your audience. The industry is always evolving, and you need to evolve with it. Keep learning and pushing your boundaries. Another thing, make sure you go to "The Namm Show," it's a must. You don't know what that is? Google it Einstein! I was asked to perform there at the "Scratch Like a Girl" showcase hosted by "Techniques" and it was life changing. I had 3 weeks to practice so I had to get my shit together big time. I bought a technique turntable and practiced until my fingers were exhausted. Reconnecting with my past mentors to get advice on how to perfect the skill of turntablism led me to scratching while wearing weights on my wrists to build strength and speed. The day of the event I flew there, performed, flew back, and had TONS of blisters on my toes. But I did it, I was cute, and I didn't die lol. My nerves were so bad since I have super stage fright that I ended up getting sick after I performed. But I didn't die. Complacency is the enemy of progress. I remember thinking I was on top of my game until I attended The Namm Show. Seeing all the new technology and innovations blew my mind and reignited my passion. It reminded me that there's always more to learn and ways to improve. I met so many legends in the industry and saw people that I knew. Stay curious and never stop learning. It's what keeps you ahead of the curve.

Don't just follow trends, set them. Innovate and elevate your craft. If you're a DJ, remix tracks in a way that nobody's heard before. If you're a host, bring new vibes and fresh ideas to your shows. Remember, the greats weren't just good at what they did, they changed the game. Be a game-changer.

Think about the legends who changed the game, Grandmaster Flash, DJ Kool Herc, & Jam Master Jay. They didn't just follow trends; they set them. They took risks and pushed boundaries. I strive to bring that same innovation to my sets. Whether it's blending unexpected genres or incorporating live elements, I aim to surprise and delight my audience. Don't be afraid to take risks and be different.

Collaboration is key. Work with other artists, producers, and creatives. It keeps your ideas fresh and your sound evolving. Plus, it opens you up to new audiences. Don't be afraid to reach out to someone who inspires you and see if they want to collaborate. You never know what kind of magic you can create together. Some of my best work has come from unexpected collaborations. Working with artists from different genres and backgrounds has expanded my horizons and brought new dimensions to my music. It's also a great way to reach new audiences. Don't limit yourself, reach out and see what kind of magic you can create together.

In the urban jungle, it's adapt or die. The music you loved five years ago might be considered old school today. Stay on top of what's hot, but don't lose your essence. Blend the new with the old and make it your own. Be a chameleon and change your colors, but never forget your stripes.

Adapting doesn't mean losing yourself. It's about blending the new with the old and making it your own. I've seen too many artists lose their identity trying to chase trends. Stay true to your roots but be open to change. It's a delicate balance, but it's essential for longevity in this industry.

Everybody talks about the hustle, but not everyone hustles smart. Work hard, but also work smart. Network, promote yourself, and build your brand. But don't just grind aimlessly. Have a plan, set goals, and make moves that get you closer to where you want to be. Remember, it's a marathon, not a sprint.

Networking is crucial in this industry. It's not just about who you know, but who knows you. Let that sink in; who knows you? Are people referring you? Is your name being mentioned in rooms that you don't occupy? Promote yourself and build your brand but do it strategically. Set goals and make moves that get you closer to where you want to be. Smart hustling is about working efficiently and effectively.

The internet is your best friend. Use it to your advantage. Social media, streaming platforms, and online communities are powerful tools. They can help you reach a global audience and keep your brand relevant. Post regularly, engage with your fans, and use analytics to see what's working and what's not. The digital age is your playground, use it wisely. Social media has changed the game. It's a powerful tool that can help you reach a global audience and keep your brand relevant. But it's not just about posting regularly; it's about engaging with your fans and using analytics to see what's working and what's not. The digital age is your playground.

Yes, this is your career, but it's also supposed to be fun. Don't take yourself too seriously. Laugh at your mistakes, enjoy the journey, and remember why you started doing this in the first place. If you're not having fun, your audience won't either.

I've had my fair share of mishaps and embarrassing moments on stage. But instead of letting them get me down, I laugh it off and keep it moving. As I write, I'm still doing a variety of things and learning. Like putting together this immense amount of knowledge that I have about the entertainment industry in a book. This is totally new to me and it's my first book. The event that I recently did was totally fucked up behind the scenes but on stage, my other crew and I made it work. One thing I will say is to the audience members attending a show, STOP looking at the DJ when things go wrong. A lot of times it's the engineer, the artists, or even the promoters...NOT the DJ. Now ya know!!!

Moving on. Your fans are your lifeline. Stay connected with them. Listen to their feedback and show them love. They're the ones who keep you going, so make sure they know you appreciate them. I make it a point to respond to messages, shout out fans at shows, and make them feel valued. After all, without them, there is no show.

Celebrate your successes, whether they're big or small. Every milestone is a step forward. Throw a party for your album release, celebrate that sold-out show, and even take a moment to appreciate the little things, like nailing a tricky mix or delivering a dope set. These moments keep you motivated and remind you why you love what you do.

While it's important to stay in the moment, don't lose sight of the long game. Think about where you want to be in five, ten, twenty years. Make decisions that will help you build a sustainable career. Invest in yourself, save money, and plan for the future. Idk about you but I highly doubt that I'm going to be an 80-year-old DJ rocking the clubs til "no-thirty" in the morning so I'm anxiously getting my retirement plan together!

Mentorship is a two-way street. Find mentors who can guide you and help you grow. At the same time, be a mentor to others. Share your knowledge and experience with up-and-coming artists. It keeps you grounded and connected to the industry's future. A great mentor of mine is DJ

Shortee, she has a wealth of information and has helped me tremendously throughout the years. I've mentored many in the industry and love passing on knowledge whenever I can. Remember, to receive blessings you must be a blessing.

Focus on building a legacy, not just chasing the next big hype. Trends come and go, but a true legacy lasts forever. Make music that matters, create experiences that people will remember, and leave your mark on the industry.

In the entertainment industry…IT'S A LOT. It's easy to lose yourself or become stagnant. But by staying true to your roots, constantly evolving, and keeping a balance, you can navigate this jungle and come out on top. Surround yourself with real people, stay hungry and curious. Remember, the journey is just as important as the destination. So, keep dropping beats, spitting bars, and living your best life honey.

Angie T:

For the most part motivation isn't the problem for me because I love the grind. It's when I've overfilled my plate and haven't had a day off in weeks that things start to get blurry. This might be tied to past trauma from when I was without, so now I work triple time to make sure that doesn't happen again, or at least that's the mentality, but I'm working on it.

I think about everything I've overcome and the people who altered their own lives to help me get here. When someone takes a chance on you, it feels like an unspoken contract, you've got to see it through. It's like a loan you repay by giving it your best. Like when I was moving to Vegas, and my friend Joe left work on short notice, called in sick, and drove 27 hours with me, even with the check engine light on (crazy, right?). I only had about $1,200 to my name at the time. I remember pulling over at a rest stop in Colorado, calling my best friend Brittany, crying, and needing her to tell me I was doing the right thing. I was so scared and shook that I actually did it, it all just hit me.

Never underestimate the amount of influence the people around you have within your life. Self motivation is important but the people you allow to speak over your life is important as well. It is crucial we be mindful who we decide to vent to and who we decide to share sensitive moments with. Had I called the wrong person in that super sensitive moment, that conversation could have very easily ended with me backing out completely and going back to the CPA job in Louisville which was the safe option. She clearly saw the light within me that my temporary moment of self-doubt wouldn't allow me to believe in and reminded me of who I am. She's the friend who believes in you before you've even fully figured out how you're going to pull it off. She reminded me of who I am! She assured me I would be ok one way or another and there was nothing to come back to. So untuck my tail and go out there and be great.

Upon arrival I had to drain most of my money on room and board, and then the stupid hair wash I bought didn't work, causing me to fail the drug test for the accounting job I was already hired for. I had to push my hustle into overdrive since the job I was counting on was no longer an option. But I wasn't ready to throw in the towel. I revamped my resume, kept applying, and finally scored a bookkeeping gig with a pyrotechnics company. Offering me the life line I desperately needed to stay in the game.

I draw strength & motivation from my family and those who came before me, and all the struggles they endured to keep pushing forward. I use that strength to help manage the current tension. Self-doubt can't overshadow the blessings right in front of you. Remember, the journey was never promised to be easy!

The F.E.W.:
DJ Kelly J, NotaboiDJ, Angie T

Even if things don't go my way depending on how dramatic it is I give myself 12-72 hours to get it all out, say my prayers and give my offerings. Then it's time to create a plan! I will admit, sometimes life throws such a tough curveball that you need some extra time to process it. That curveball is called grief. Just hearing or seeing the word is enough to make you sit up straight. I lost my hero, my Great Grandfather and 3 months later the love of my life in the midst of pursuing my career and it was the hardest comeback I tried to make in my life.

Having to rebuild myself mentally, physically, emotionally & spiritually being thousands of miles away from my family was a battle I didn't realize I'd overcome. See in this industry it's 1% of how you feel and 99% of how you make the customers feel. Any personal issues need to be left in the car or at your house. It'll be waiting on you as soon as you're done. I didn't want to work, I didn't want to talk, couldn't stop randomly crying at the slightest memory trigger. I recall having a conversation with NAB about the random spouts of extreme sadness with tears and she warned me that it will be a while before that goes away. I was looking for a fast track to healing because there's no way I would survive this heartbreak if I had to experience it any longer.

What really hit me were the pitying looks and those moments when people offered condolences in a way that felt more intrusive than supportive. Almost as if they saw the pain and wanted to offer sympathy. At the moment, I would've preferred if they had just kept their comments to themselves and not looked into my aching soul. In retrospect, I understand that these people had been through something similar and know that pain all too familiar. It was their way of showing empathy, and in a way that there will be better days, just keep pushing. Grief can sometimes cross wires in your brain and have you trippin for real, but shutting people out won't help you heal.

What still confuses me, though, is why random people thought it was okay to talk about the loss while I was in the middle of hosting an event. I remember someone walking up to me in the club saying "OMG Angie T I'm so sorry that this happened, if it was me I would be a mess! I wouldn't be able to get out of bed, I would just be destroyed. Like what happened?" And in this moment I remember feeling like IKYFL combined with a feeling of deep sadness followed by omg don't cry don't cry don't cry. I let it go with a "It's crazy" comment with hopes of no follow up questions or comments because I wasn't sure if I'd just burst into tears or curse her ass out for being (unintentionally) insensitive.

I think people look at us like robots or just assume life is always lit we're just hanging out having fun and it's not a job. It was a lot to balance, but I have to say the people around me definitely held me up in ways I've never needed before. From my friends jumping into action & taking my calls/text to let everyone know I was ok and that I just need space, to once the funeral was over, finding ways to keep me uplifted while being a listening ear even if I told the same story 2-3 times before. Though it hurt, I think one of the biggest ways I got through it was by 'TALKING ABOUT IT' all the memories, from the big moments to the small, intimate ones that stood out the most.

I'm also so thankful for my counselor, who met with me and helped me find myself in the midst of it all. It was all hands on deck for a while. It took me some time before I could visit back home in KY, where I was overwhelmed with memories of my grandfather and my love everywhere I went. That doesn't mean I don't still have moments (like now), but I'm not stuck in the rut I once was. This was a time when I had some real out-of-body experiences and had to relearn myself.

I changed the way I ate. I changed the way I dressed from the colors that I picked for the day. I changed the way I allow people to talk to me. I changed the way that I talked to other people and I try to do more listening than talking. Through my counseling sessions, I learned that a lot of time, women carry our stress in our womb area (sacral chakra) and I had never done a cleanse before. Shit, I'd never heard of stretching to release built up trauma either. I learned that your childhood experiences are a direct reflection of how you interact with people today and until you address it you will continue to be in that cycle. I learned how to listen to my body and how it reacts to certain situations. For instance, if I'm discussing something and start to feel pain, if I experience a sensation in my chest or tingling in my foot, it's usually a sign that something around me is affecting me. I think we're often used to ignoring these signals, but as I rebuilt myself, I learned to recognize them. This is how my body communicates with me—my intuition feels like a superpower.

In the beginning, I was furious. I was angry at everyone, even God. This is what led me to embark on my own spiritual journey. I began researching my spiritual, mental, and physical growth because I'd never felt this way before. I needed to understand why my grandfather passed away the moment my flight landed in KY and why I couldn't make it to the hospital in time. I needed to understand why God let me and my love get so close to closing the gap, only to rip it away from me. The same God who's protected me all this time wouldn't destroy me now, right? Everything happens for a reason, even if I don't like, agree or want to accept it.

In time I started patting myself on the back on the days that went by, and I wouldn't cry. A song, scent or picture that would trigger a memory, would no longer make me ball into tears. It wasn't overnight, but it was a gradual thing, so with this information, I now have a deeper understanding of people. When I host events, I always keep in mind that someone could be going through a similar struggle, perhaps giving themselves a pep talk before stepping into the venue to hold it together. With that in mind, I see it as my duty to ensure they have a great time, or at least try my best for everyone. This experience has helped me understand people better and deepened my empathy. So, if you're going through something right now, no matter where you are in your journey, I'm proud of you! Even if all you managed today was taking a shower and making your bed, I'm proud of you! Seeing people enjoy themselves feeds my spirit. I refuse to let the industry strip away or exploit my talent and take away the genuine joy I get from making others happy.

Kelly J:

As far as not losing myself, I definitely went astray a few times, lol. My run-ins with imposter syndrome were short lived, in part because I always had support in some way. Somebody was always there to help me get out of my own way. A friend, a stranger, a random message from someone cheering me on, maybe my grandmother sending the troops per usual. A family member or friend may say anything to make you feel better, but a complete stranger cheering you on hits different. A gig that was super random but SO much fun and issue-free regarding payment. The few times I felt alone, I didn't allow myself to sit in loneliness long enough to get stuck. I'd force myself to go out and be around people I loved. Or see something that made me laugh. Comedy shows have been a "fix" of mine for over a decade, and one of the many reasons why I love friends like AK. Or I was always reminded of the battle scars I had to prove the validity of my position, and it helped that I rarely doubted my skill set. I had "damn that set was trash" days, but rarely "hang the turntables and headphones up" days. This confidence of work-related things started with a confidence of school-related things when I was a kid, and even though I was far from a school desk, the mindset to get up and go be whatever I want has always outweighed fear. Oh but my body….

I learned how to listen to my body and how it reacts to certain situations. – **Ang**

I think the older we get and the more connected we are to ourselves, the more our bodies will talk to us when things are wrong. This proved to be the case for me, and one time, Ang and NAB caught the signs before I did.

I was in a not-so-great period of a relationship and my body was starting to shut down, literally. Working out had become a norm since Z was born, but by this time, I hadn't figured out a consistent schedule within the schedule of my relationship and work. My body wasn't happy. It got to a point where my back had completely locked up. The only other time I experienced pain like that was when I was overworking myself in my early 20s and fractured my ribs (still don't exactly know how that happened). I wasn't sure if it was a pinched nerve or what, but alongside my mood and my aura to others, my body was telling me to switch things up, quick! I just wasn't listening.

I was still working consistently; DJ Kelly J was okay. But Kelly was going through it! Sometimes we have guardian angels, living and spiritually. I have Ang and NAB (idk if they're angels, JK). They literally popped up at my house one morning. Early af, banging on the door, they were both there and said it was time to go. My boyfriend was there, but he wasn't about to go back and forth with them either. He helped me pack and off we went.

We talked about this trip a few times but never officially made plans. Sedona is a spot in Arizona, near Phoenix, known to have strong spiritual properties. Hiking trips there can be incredibly healing, if not life changing altogether. There are four vortexes found there that focus on healing, meditation, and self-exploration. We needed ALL of that shit. After the 4-hour drive, the foodie in us took over. We found this fire Mexican restaurant, grabbed food and margaritas. We needed to beat the sun, so immediately after, we started our hike, and soaked it all in. When we got to the top of our trail, we stopped for a little while to meditate. I couldn't let myself cry but I wanted to. My back was still hurting so bad that I couldn't stand up completely straight, but I did start to get relief. I knew that when I got back to Vegas, some drastic changes needed to be made, otherwise I'd lose myself completely.

The F.E.W.:
DJ Kelly J, NotaboiDJ, Angie T

I mentioned before that I always get signs when I'm messing up or need to change things, and honestly, I believe that everyone does. You'll get some kind of sign before shit completely hits the fan. A good village, some self-awareness and action works wonders. MOVE!

I know now that a consistent exercise routine is mandatory for me. Alongside the physical benefits, it's the only time I have to myself and my own thoughts. My own wants and needs. Any relationship getting in the way of that is bound to lead to chaos.

NAB:

The trip was amaze - balls & those margaritas were to die for (literally). We all had different needs for going to Sedona because I needed to find a Native American statue to purchase but never did. Oh, and we ended the hike expeditiously when a swarm of mosquitoes came to annihilate us. Nonetheless, it was a memory that I'll always hold near and dear to my heart.

Angie T:

It's funny how we all remember and experience shit differently. I can laugh about it now but I was fired UP at these heffas for ordering big plates of

179

chimichangas and bottomless margaritas right before our hike. Not to mention NAB wanted to stop at some of the local shops to look for a statue and all I wanted to do was hike and get my Zen on in the eye of the vortex. But like NAB mentioned the mosquitoes attacked us as soon as I felt centered, it was time to roll. Funny part is we went back to the shopping area after the hike, I had a vivid Deja vu moment of a dream I had previously. I always look at these moments as confirmation that I am exactly where I'm supposed to be, so maybe the mosquitoes where saving me from sudden death after all.

TRACK 6:
Sky Is The Limit
The Come Up

Angie T:

I'll never forget my first time attending a networking event alone. I spent a lot of time trying to get friends to join me, but everyone had their reasons for not being able to make it. So, I decided right then and there to go by myself and just make it happen. I was so nervous that I sat in my car for a while, trying to pump myself up. I called my best friend Brit for a pep talk because my stomach was in knots. I was ready to start my car & reverse the hell out of there! Overthinking like a mf! After our call, we came up with a game plan: I'd head to the bar first to get some wine and start my first conversation there. It turned out to be a pretty solid strategy for networking solo. At the time, I was a tax preparer/brand ambassador for a tax company, while also doing bookkeeping for a CPA firm so my services were an easy thing to sell. Before long, I had made several new connections and even landed an interview on the News to talk about taxes.

I was so excited and shocked at what I was able to achieve from just jumping out there. I knew after that I could really do anything I put my mind to! So, reader, yes YOU, I wanna tell you to do it.

Do it scared, do it unsure, do it until ya satisfied...
DO IT!

Your next opportunity is probably on the other side of the thing that makes you scared. And let me tell you, whoever's trying to keep you under their thumb is counting on you to stay scared and unmotivated. So what will you do?!

Whenever I attend events, I set a simple goal for myself, whether it's collecting a certain number of business cards, making Instagram connections, getting phone numbers or email addresses, or finding new donors or volunteers for the non-profit. Once you get past the nerves of networking solo, the next challenge is the follow-up. After collecting 17 business cards, what good are they if you don't reach out to the people you met? It might sound simple, but following up can low-key feel like a part-time job. Think about it. You meet someone, collect their info with the promise of contacting them, and then move on to meet another person and do it all over again multiple times at one event. The next day, or whenever you have time to review the cards, you need to remember each person, what you discussed, and what your follow-up should be. It's important to remember your goals and the purpose behind your networking. Being mindful of these goals will make it easier to manage your connections and ensure you're networking with intention!

Even with that plan, I still can't be the only person to talk about and promote my services. Once I realized that many of my opportunities come from my own resources, like the people who enjoy my hosting and keep coming to my events, I understood that these connections are also key to my next ventures. In this industry, ego often drives people, and many aren't comfortable asking for their price, seeking help, or asking for anything at all. I used to be one of those people, but not anymore, I'm asking! The funny thing is, nine times out of ten, the people I've reached out to were more than happy and willing to help. It turns out it was all just in my head. Noticing a pattern here?

Starting out on internet radio in Vegas, I would go and network at community events, on the strip, in the casino, everywhere. There was a time I went walking down the strip to promote my internet radio show and to see if I would possibly meet someone interesting enough to interview on my show. I stopped a girl who was also there passing out flyers and we started talking about what she was promoting.

My mind immediately went to sponsorship. She was promoting a party bus that would run up and down the strip, so she passed along the contact info for the owners and I told her I'd follow up with them. I reached out to set up a meeting and we had a call to go over the details of the business. He had let me know that they weren't looking for sponsorships but if I wanted to start a promo code and send people over I'd get a kick back.

At this point they had only been on business for about a year so they were hustling just like I was. He had invited me to come on a tour, so me and my homegirl went on a tour and we had a BALL! The tour starts at a bar on the strip, next you go into the club, then the party bus where you can also bring a bottle of your choice (they provided liquor for you as well) and then they would drop you off to the last club. By the end of the tour, he offered me the opportunity to be a host for the party bus. Jumping into this role was like diving into the deep end of the nightlife scene. I was responsible for everything: checking in customers, helping them get into the club, DJing and bartending on the party bus, and ensuring everyone made it to the last club. This hands-on experience was a crash course in reading people's music tastes and adapting to a diverse crowd. Dealing with drunk people? Just as stubborn as sober folks, if not more! With a mix of people from all over the world, adaptability was key. I may not have a turntable but I can plug my aux cord in real quick and get the party going. It's funny cause I still have the playlist on my Spotify titled Party Bus juuuust in case.

I'd continue to do independent gigs until the opportunity I prayed for came along... Brunch! After hosting the nightclubs & party buses for so many years, I yearned for a change. I wanted to do something during the day. So, when the opportunity came to me, I jumped on it and as of right now I host one of the hottest Brunch experiences anyone has ever attended. This all came to be because, first of all, I asked God for it! Second, I stayed active in the community, which kept me on people's radar. By showing my face, participating however I could, and collaborating when it made sense, I made sure people remembered to book me when the opportunity arose. My number was finally called. I'd be lying if

I said there weren't any doubters. Some people didn't believe in my capabilities and I know this because they told me once the doubts were cleared. There will always be someone with a turned-up nose (let them stay mad) I'm still out here winning!

I'd say Las Vegas has a tight-knit scene, but honestly, it's the industry itself that defines it. There's a core group of people who come together for events, concerts, and festivals. When your name comes up, you want to ensure that the one person in the room who's defending you can genuinely back you up with positive things. Keeping your brand clean and avoiding unnecessary drama makes it easier for them to stand up for you with real & good things to say. Let's be honest. Not everyone will be your fan, and that's just part of it. What matters is staying true to your path and trusting that your tribe (supporters) will find you.

Be wary of those who might try to dim your light. Promoters can try to use opportunities as a means of trying to control you. Community events might not always be paid gigs, but they're invaluable for gaining experience. Whether you're hosting, DJing, or involved in any part of entertainment, you need to get out there and practice. Know that you have a place and keep pushing forward.

Kelly J:

I would DJ forever if I could determine the frequency. The creative space is constantly growing, and DJs are able to do a lot more than before, so in the right space, I feel a lot of DJs would do so until their last breath. But the environment can and does influence your growth, or lack of.

For example, if you're a club hopper or in an area where you only see DJs in nightclubs, you may not immediately know that DJs are just about EVERYWHERE. Clubs, lounges, stores, weddings, the radio, community events, political events, literally everywhere. Knowing all of the possibilities of djing, and how to DJ in each of them, because they're NOT all the same, will not only keep you busy, but allow more creative opportunities while at work. I was fortunate enough to begin my DJ career in Las Vegas, and had mentorship or direction in just about all of the different avenues. This may not exactly be the case in every city, but the energy put into researching it can prove to be more beneficial than not. It's important to keep in mind that maneuvering through each avenue has its own trials and tribulations, so you gotta put your big girl panties/

big boy drawers on in some cases, as you can already see in some of our experiences.

Some experiences are truly a case-by-case basis, your case may not be my case, my case may not be NAB's case. I go with my gut most times, and although I've had some tough losses, I truly believe that some, definitely not all, opportunities are worth the risk. Learning from your or even my mistakes is a huge plus though!

I remember desperately wanting to go, ANYWHERE. Wanting to meet new people, DJ in new places, like yesterday. Around this time, I was mapping out my life as a new single mom, trying to fix my credit and see what life for Z and I would look like. I needed a newer car, and although I started a savings for Z and I, I was living with my mom and uncle, and knew I couldn't do so forever. I would wake up around 5am every day. Even if I just got home at 2am. I kinda had to, because Z would wake up around 6:30/7am, so if I needed alone time, or time to work on mixes, graphics, even to go through emails, I needed to do it before she was up. I did some research on Instagram, even doing some side by sides on Facebook, looking for traveling groups. I stumbled across BlackOutWeekend, an urban professionals event series of about 10 events within 4 days in Lake

The F.E.W.:
DJ Kelly J, NotaboiDJ, Angie T

Tahoe, CA/NV. Mind you this event takes place in MARCH, in the SNOW. Yes, I willingly chose to leave the desert to party in some snow! It looked like SO much fun!

I shot my shot.

I found the event coordinator and founder's email, sent her my EPK and expressed to her that I'd be an asset on the team. She actually responded to my email! The first year, they paid for my hotel and travel only; this was basically my audition to show what I can do and see how I mesh with the already established team consisting of some of the best DJs from all over the country. It was literally as fun as it looked on Instagram! From meeting the team, to interacting with the partygoers that included black doctors, lawyers, entrepreneurs, and basically people that had sh*t to lose that knew how to behave themselves and have a good time, y'all I didn't want to leave! The following years, my travel, hotel, and pay included, and I earned a resident spot on the BlackOutWeekend team.

Another dope opportunity happened some years later. I crossed paths with a really dope DJ, Miss Joy, a vet in the industry that I looked up to for years. We had only seen each other maybe 2-3 times ever, and actually have pictures for each moment, but we never really got the opportunity to talk to each other until recently. We were djing in the same casino and she passed the venue I was at in her route to her venue. I asked her to be a guest speaker at my DJ workshop, and she agreed, which I'm still eternally grateful for. Sometime later, I attended an event of hers, and she connected me to the owner of one of the agencies in Las Vegas that book the DJs on the world-famous Fremont Street Experience. The energy at the event was so dope, like with everybody there.

The owner of the agency offered to give me an opportunity to spin on the stage, not with opening set, but middle set, and the pay was good. Winner winner chicken dinner! There was one catch though; this set was an EDM/dance set, and as of now, I had maybe done a set like this two times in my entire career. Yikes! There was no turning back.

I researched my butt off and practiced some sets at home. But to my surprise, I enjoyed making these kinds of sets, a LOT. When the day finally came for me to spin on the Fremont Street Experience stage, I was beyond nervous. You see people from all walks of life downtown, and I do mean ALL walks of life. Sometimes it's hard to handle, especially when it's thousands of people.

The F.E.W.:
DJ Kelly J, NotaboiDJ, Angie T

But man, when you see that wave of people dancing to YOUR music, that feeling takes over your soul! It felt so good just seeing people dancing and having a good time. It had been a while since I had seen people just not care about what others are thinking or doing, and just had fun. I had thanked the owner of the agency a million times over for the experience, and they continue to book me periodically to this day.

"Luck is when preparation meets opportunity." People think I'm lucky af, and they're only partially right. When an opportunity comes, I rarely say no, lol, whether I am prepared for it or not. The magic lies in how strongly I believe in myself, how clearly I see my goals, and how those things overpower fear. I'm not scary and I'm gonna figure some sh*t out, because I believe in myself. I think the Universe gives you what you want, and people don't realize that they are so focused on the things that they DON'T want, that the Universe thinks you're asking for it. Mindset is at the forefront yet again, and although you can't prepare for everything, there are small things you can do to curb the blows and make the best out of the most random opportunity.

I'll never forget one of the last gigs I had and Coolio was the headliner. It was in one of the most respected venues in downtown Las Vegas, and the client's theme was the curve ball I could've NEVER guessed. This was a very high-profile gig, that a mentor referred me for. The theme was medieval times. And they wanted medieval music blended with hip-hop! I didn't bat an eye y'all. I told them how dope it was and that I'd work on a set. Tell me why I found an entire catalog of hip-hop songs with medieval versions! The client was so impressed, and so was I after that night, lol. It was really dope catching a live performance by Coolio before his untimely passing too.

I definitely have some advice: practice whenever you get free time. Real DJs still crate dig. Crate digging is looking for music or versions of songs that aren't widely known or played. More than ever, a lot of DJs are making their own remixes. Turn the tv off, put the video games down, put your phone down and lowkey put it in another room, so you can focus. I don't really get free time at home, so most times I'm doing a radio mix, or even a club set, I get there early enough to try out new songs. This is why I seldomly like when people try to have a conversation while I'm djing. Or, in certain public places like a gym or the store, I'm listening to the music that's playing. "Do I have this song? Oh damn, this was a banger back in the day! Let me see if I can find a good remix or make one." My car time is a big one. I'm either listening to the radio or complete silence, and no I'm not crazy. DJs listen to music whenever they're at work, and guess who's always working? When I'm off, and don't have Z asking for the same 5 songs whenever she's in the car, sometimes I need complete silence. I need to reset my thoughts, clear my head of the songs I played, and give myself a fresh start for the next gig. Or remember that I need to go to the grocery store or get an oil change for my car. On the other hand, I go through multiple radio stations just to see what they're playing. Like ALL of the genres though. Jazz, rock, country, hip hop, r&b, to see if I need to add something to my library. The radio stations still have their feet in the industry enough to know what's trending in each genre. So, if it's on the radio and you don't have it, you probably need to get it.

Working out is another big one and I mentioned it earlier. Women in the industry will always have their image play a factor into their brand, and although I personally never wish to be smaller than a size 7 ever, I know I better slow down on eating late and make sure my butt is in the gym a few times a week. I've randomly gotten brand endorsements, big gigs, and tv opportunities. If I wasn't in the gym at all when these opportunities came, I'd be pissed at myself. All of this is preparation.

Super notable mention: I have a whole DJ workshop at UNLV! To be transparent, I wasn't on board with teaching anything at first, and for a few reasons, that imposter syndrome made another guest appearance around this time. I was offered this opportunity years before while still at 88.1 FM, and it definitely didn't make sense then. I wasn't "on." I was financially all over the place and still trying to get my foundation right. My skills were okay, not at a pro level to be teaching somebody. I felt if I wasn't as dope as Jazzy Jeff, I shouldn't be teaching.

Plus, this offer wanted me to charge people to take the class. None of my mentors charged me to teach me what they knew, so to charge people for what they taught me, didn't feel right. The momentum from then till 2021 was a LOT different, though. It's something about being a single mom that really pushed me to just start kicking down doors and figuring things out regarding being a DJ professionally. Or maybe it was really all of the previous years of grinding finally bearing fruit. Maybe it was both. My career, my skill set, my brand, was in a much different place. (It needs to be said that I'm still not on the level of DJ Jazzy Jeff, I did finally get to meet him though!) So, when the opportunity came back, this time to teach at UNLV, I took it, making sure that it could remain free for people to take. I built a curriculum from the ground up, tweaking it every time there are changes in the industry, and have the workshop every Fall and Spring on campus. It was initially 10 weeks long, which is shorter than most classes, but available to anyone, whether you're a UNLV student or not, as long as you're at least 16 years old. Once the word got out, the class took off. It expanded from one, to two classes every Fall and Spring, with support from not only the top DJs in Las Vegas, but brands such as BPM Music, Serato and Mixcloud. Nobody, not even my future self, could've told me at 19 when I dropped out of UNLV to be a DJ that I'd be right back there in my 30s teaching. And a DJ workshop at that! 3 years into it, and other colleges and universities have inquired about me bringing the workshop over to them. Another opportunity I would've never dreamed of.

Fast forward, I've DJed for just about everybody, no exaggeration. Just about all the casinos, all the clubs, all the companies, big and small, now diving into sports. Because I didn't give myself a plan B, my plan A was always strong, with my full effort. I've been blessed to travel, take Z with me to gigs both locally, and out of state. Because of her village, she's been to more states than I have actually. I get to do what I love, pass my wisdom on to the next wave, raise my child with more flexibility than most, and invest inter-generationally into my family, which is the biggest blessing of all for me.

NAB:

Yo, the entertainment industry is wild, man. It's like one big, never-ending party where opportunities pop up like confetti. I started from the bottom, spinnin records at a local fitness gym. Back then, I was just hoping the neighbors wouldn't call the cops on us. Fast forward a bit, and now I'm rocking high-profile events, from lit festivals to corporate gigs that pay damn near better than my last tax return. It's crazy how things change when you put in the work and know how to keep a crowd hype.

At first I was gigging any and everywhere that would let me. In case you didn't know, this is a male dominated industry. It's getting better but we've still got a long way to go. Did you know...the 75 top highest paid DJ'S are male? Why are only 13% of songwriters and 3% of producers on top songs women? Why do women in entertainment face higher rates of anxiety, depression, and burnout? What in the entire fuck? Well, they say you have to pay your dues and in MY opinion, that's what I did. Some events were volunteer and free but the only thing that mattered is that people heard me. According to some more seasoned industry goofies, I moved up the ladder unfairly faster than most, but when something is for you who can be against you? They'll be naysayers and those who question your moves but you have to stay true to yourself. I promise you will go far in life if you focus on attracting, not chasing. I started Djing in July 2018 and said I would go full time and leave corporate America in 3 years, but the "Scamdemic" put a halt to that. In 2022, I believed that since Vegas had reopened, opportunities were pouring in, & the radio station had asked me to be the morning show DJ Mon-Fri (initially I had begun working there some Friday evenings) it was time. An extra year was added to my plans but I officially retired in July of 2022, and never looked back (well almost never lol). If you set realistic goals for yourself that have deadlines you will reach them or give up on them, one or the other has to happen for growth. Some of my favorite words start with the letter "D", not the trendy "demure" or "diabolical" words but "DISCIPLINE"! It's crucial to have lots of it. Remember you can always start over, just START!

One of the dopest opportunities I've snagged is teaming up with big names like Harry Reid International Airport. I mean, who would've thought? These partnerships are more than just about getting that bag; they're about merging vibes and reaching new crowds. With the airport, we were giving away swag bags, connecting with people all over the world, and creating exclusive content. It's like a dream collab where the world meets beats, plus having my name associated with a major establishment. That's a whole new level of street cred.

And let's talk about media exposure. Yo, when you're the DJ for a morning show on a radio station, you know you're onto something. Media shout-outs are clutch for building your brand. It's one thing to be killing it at gigs but when the media catches on and starts hyping you up, that's when you know you've arrived. Each interview or guest spot is a chance to connect with more fans and tell your story. It's like adding another layer to the hustle.

Networking, man, that's the secret sauce. Every gig, every event, it's all about who you meet. I've rubbed elbows with some of everyone in the game, and those connections are priceless. It's like having a VIP pass to the best opportunities. From finding new gigs to getting advice from industry vets, your network is your net worth. The entertainment world might seem huge, but it's tight-knit, and building those relationships are essential.

This industry gives you a platform, and using it to make a difference is what it's all about. With the radio station, we're able to promote scholarships, organize community projects, and mentor the youth. It's not just about the music and the parties; it's about using our influence to uplift and support. Seeing the impact we can make is better than any paycheck. Juneteenth events are the absolute best. If I could just do concerts and festivals, that would make all of my wettest dreams come true. The station does these festivals annually and I get to DJ for the masses. There's multiple events and thousands of people there that actually come to have a good time. I meet so many people that approach me and say they listen to me on the radio every morning. This will never get old. Idk if I'll ever get used to those that notice me in public, at a restaurant, or a gym. But I am truly grateful.

Another event that I did with the Medical Marijuana for Minorities was one for the books. It was an upscale event in which I got to DJ alongside "Redman". Did you hear me? REDMAN! Ok, now

BARS & BEATS

I will tell you as a kid Puff Daddy & Redman were my mf FAVS so this opportunity was one where I had to not act starstruck. And ya girl held it together but babyyyyy that shit was dope. He had me come to his and Method Man's concert the next day, backstage access and all. Needless to say, he's the coolest cat ever and we've built a pretty good friendship since then over the years. I even send him some of my "Super Natural Nia" Organic Teas every now and then! He's probably do for some more by now, but that's the homie real talk.

Staying educated is crucial. The game is always changing, and you gotta keep up. I'm always reading, hitting up seminars, and online courses to stay ahead. Whether it's new tech, industry trends, or just brushing up on the business side of things, staying informed keeps me sharp. The industry thrives on innovation, and I'm all about being the one setting trends, not following them.

One of the best parts of this journey is inspiring and being inspired. The entertainment world is a melting pot of creativity. Every gig, every event, I meet people who push me to step up my game. And knowing that I can inspire others is the icing on the cake. Whether it's through my sets, my collabs, or my community work, seeing the impact of what I do is the ultimate reward.

The F.E.W.:
DJ Kelly J, NotaboiDJ, Angie T

The cash flow has definitely leveled up since the early days. Back then, it was about hustling for every dollar, sometimes getting paid in exposure— which, let's be real, doesn't pay the bills. But once you start making a name for yourself, the money starts to roll in. High-profile gigs and brand partnerships, Cha-ching! It's like leveling up in a game, where every move you make gets you closer to the big rewards. It's not just about making money though; it's about making smart moves with it. Investing back into your craft, upgrading equipment, and even saving for those rainy days. Trust, having a solid financial plan is just as crucial as having a killer playlist.

Another opportunity that's come my way is mentorship. As you climb the ladder, people start looking up to you. I've had the chance to mentor up-and-coming DJs, kids, and artists, sharing the knowledge I've picked up along the way. It's a great way to give back and ensure the next generation of talent has the tools they need to succeed. Plus, it keeps me on my toes, reminding me of where I started and how far I've come.

I'm a huge Afrobeat lover and it's no secret. The radio station told me to connect with "The House of Blues", to see if I could DJ for Adekunle

Gold. SHOOT YOUR SHOT! I've never had to sell myself or ask for gigs other than the ones that I really wanted. Just like the airport, I reached out via email in the most professional way and they gave me a chance. Since I'm not getting on nobody's Mic I called Angie T and the rest is history.

Being recognized by the industry is another sweet perk. Awards and accolades are great for the ego, sure, but they also validate the grind. They open doors and get you noticed by people who might not have been paying attention before. Plus, it feels good to get that pat on the back and know that your hard work is being seen and appreciated. Being at the radio station has been pivotal with that!

Technology has been a massive boost too. Staying on top of the latest gear and software keeps my sets fresh and exciting. It's not just about knowing how to mix anymore; it's about creating an experience. Visuals, lights, and effects all play a part in making a performance unforgettable. Being tech-savvy gives you an edge and helps you stand out in a crowded field. Everytime I get some extra bread, I'm trying to see what I can add to my collection. From backup laptops, controllers, turntables, speakers, etc., I just keep buying lol.

The F.E.W.:
DJ Kelly J, NotaboiDJ, Angie T

And let's not forget the fun. Yeah, it's a lot of hard work, but it's also a blast. The adrenaline rush of performing live, seeing people lose themselves in the music, that's what it's all about. It's those moments that make all the hustle worth it. The late nights, the early mornings, the travel, it all fades away when you're in the zone, doing what you love.

So yeah, the entertainment industry is a wild ride, full of opportunities if you're ready to grab them. From high-profile gigs to killer collaborations, media exposure, and giving back, it's all a part of the hustle. And trust me, the journey's just getting started. Here's to more beats, more vibes, and more success. Let's get it!

BARS & BEATS

TRACK 7:
Waterfalls
Rhythm and Restraint

NAB:

This is probably one of the hardest things to manage in the industry. Being a DJ in the entertainment game is wild, but self-discipline is what keeps you on top. People think it's all late-night parties (I mean it kinda is), but there's a lot more to it. If you want to be successful and not strung out, you gotta have discipline. Imagine…every time you show up there's SHOTS. I mean E-V-E-R-Y-T-I-M-E. It's like people don't even think that you could possibly want some H20 or may be a little famished. Why are yall like this? From now on when you hire a DJ, make sure that mf got some water. OK?! And DJ, whenever you have a gig be sure to bring water with you in case the fools hiring you lack the decency to give you some. Oh, and we like tips instead of drinks too!!!

First off, you gotta practice regularly. DJing isn't just about playing tracks; it's about perfecting your transitions, knowing your beats, and creating mixes that vibe with the crowd. This means putting in the hours every week, no matter how busy you are. Self-discipline is making sure you stick to that practice schedule. I DJ about 6-7 days a week and if you can do basic math, then you can see how challenging it is for me to practice. Between my kids, my cat, my tea business (www.supernaturalnia.com), and ME, where's the time to DJ? It doesn't matter, at the end of the day you must practice. Even if you don't sleep!

This industry is hella competitive. To stay relevant, you need to keep your music library updated, know the latest trends, and adapt to what the audience wants. This means spending a lot of time researching and listening to new tracks. You need to manage your time well and be disciplined enough to keep up with everything. Having a backup of everything is clutch. Currently, I'm re-downloading songs because for some stupid reason, I lost thousands of songs. It might take me the rest of my life to recover that music but oh well…it is what it is.

Taking care of your health is another big one. Late nights can mess with your sleep and lead to unhealthy habits. Self-discipline means making sure you get enough rest, eat right, and work out. This keeps you in good shape and your mind sharp, which is crucial when you're performing. It's all about finding that balance so you can keep going strong, both on and off the stage. Tricky, tricky, tricky. It's so annoying that I'm offered shots and drinks at pretty much every event I attend. So, if you remember how much I work, add in some drinks, and the fact that this is Las Vegas, then my friend that's a huge CATASTROPHE. Over the years I started incorporating healthier habits into my lifestyle. I barely drink cuz I spent many moons laid out on the bathroom floor throwing up and promising to never indulge again. Meat is of little to no consumption, plus I exercise, and take hella supplements. Still the temptation can be a bit overwhelming sometimes…plus we're all human. Right?

Networking is huge in this industry, but it takes discipline to do it right. It's easy to get caught up in the party scene, but you have to stay professional. This means being on time, reliable, and having a good attitude. Discipline in how you handle yourself helps you build a solid reputation, that will open up more opportunities. Being able to portray yourself in a professional manner is pivotal in trying to stand out. So many people in the industry lack basic good work ethics, and at the end of the day this is a business which means you've gotta play the part.

Money management is another area where you need discipline. DJ income can be all over the place, depending on how many gigs you get and the time of year. You gotta be smart with your money, saving up during the good times and investing in quality gear. Don't blow your cash on stuff you don't need. Financial discipline ensures you're stable for the long run. Some weeks you may be booked daily while others there's a huge drought. You have got to know how to balance your finances, or else you will drown. Having a retirement fund is something that has to be planned without the assistance of a day-to-day company that will contribute on a monthly basis. From the get-go, start saving at least 15% of all of your income and you will thank me later!

Finally, you need discipline to set and stick to your boundaries. The entertainment world can blur lines, so knowing your limits is key. Sometimes, this means turning down gigs that don't match your values or making sure you have downtime to recharge. When it comes to volunteering, you've got to be willing to give back. We all started somewhere, so don't forget that everyone needs a helping hand. Some nonprofit organizations are good ways to fulfill this obligation as long as you have a cap. There's a limit to what you should offer, and people will definitely try to take advantage of your services if you give them away too easily.

In the end, being someone with self-discipline is about balancing the fun and chaos of the job with a structured approach to practice, health, networking, and money management. It's this discipline that keeps you successful and feeling good in the fast-paced world of entertainment. Your job is a business and everything you do represents your brand.

Even the things that you post on social media affects your image and what you're trying to build. Be private and particular about the things that you share, because once it's out, it can't come back in. Your online presence is part of your brand, so keep it clean and professional. The less you say, the less you'll have to explain. Who wants to have to explain to a potential client that you were just going through some things? Not a good look. TSK TSK TSK. Now vice control!

The music, the energy, and late-night parties are all part of the gig. But let's keep it real, it's not all glitz and glam. There are plenty of pitfalls that can mess with your game if you're not careful. Vice control is key, and if you don't master it, you can kiss your career goodbye. Did I mention that this is Sin City? I mean you can get into so much trouble out here it's ridiculous. Anything or anyone you want can be had at a simple beckoning call. You most certainly gotta keep your shit in order!

First off, the party scene is a beast. Free drinks, VIP access, and all that is tempting to dive in headfirst. But here's the thing: moderation is your best friend. Too much booze or any other substance, and you're looking at a slippery slope. It's cool to have a drink or two but know your limit. Decide beforehand how much you're gonna drink and stick to it. And for real, drink water. Alcohol dehydrates you and leaves you feeling like trash. Keep a bottle of water handy and stay hydrated. As if being a desert isn't enough, when you've gotta get up at 5am Mon-Fri for the radio show that you DJ for, you've gotta make different choices. When I first got into this lifestyle, I had a different view of how I needed to conduct myself. I worked a regular 9-5 and I didn't need to self-regulate so much when it came to vices. In 2022, I retired from corporate America to DJ full time and run my tea business (what's it called?) (www.supernaturalnia.com lol).

That was a whole new monster I had to tackle since I wasn't used to needing to be so in control of my habits. There was no way that I could drink as much and let's be clear, I only drink hard liquor on the rocks or with soda water (so I don't have to worry about calories). Besides, I can't risk having to run to the bathroom all night pissing like a racehorse from drinking wine and beer. Straight to the point with me…I digress. Moral of the story, you have to be mindful of what vices take you out of character and make you feel like death. Performing is the number 1 objective in this industry so be sure to not indulge in anything that's going to compromise that.

Healthy habits are your secret weapon. Late nights and early mornings can wreck your body if you're not careful. Get in some exercise, eat right, and make sure you're catching enough Z's. This lifestyle can take a toll, but if you keep your body in check, you'll have the stamina to keep rocking those gigs. And don't let peer pressure get to you. Know your limits and surround yourself with people who respect your choices. Baby, if late nights and early mornings was an industry…

VIOLA. There's no real way to just take on gigs that will be at a reasonable time and allow you the proper sleep that you need, so just be prepared. Some days you won't be able to cater to your healthier choices and you'll be all over the place. All I can say is, "Rest when you can!" It is integral.

Rest is one of the biggest things we overlook when trying to get to the bag and it can cost you EVERYTHING. I've had my share of dehydrations, sleep deprivation, starvation, auto immune, etc. in this industry to know better. Unfortunately, I had to learn all of this on my own (the hard way). When you can sleep DO IT, when you can't PRAY!!!

Stress is another biggie in this game. High-pressure gigs, tight schedules, and the constant hustle can get overwhelming. You gotta have ways to chill out and manage that stress. Meditation and mindfulness can help you stay grounded. They'll keep your head clear and help you handle the pressure without falling into bad habits. Make sure you're not overloading your schedule. Balance your gigs with enough downtime to recharge. And if things get too heavy, don't be afraid to talk to a therapist.

They can give you strategies to cope without turning to vices. Therapy is the cheat code. I mean this industry is as unorthodox as it gets, and stress goes unregulated for years to the point of exhaustion. Taking the time to turn your phone off and do absolutely nothing is quite daunting but a liberating experience. What I've learned to do most days when I wake up is stretch and pray for 5 minutes each, every morning. It's only 10 minutes but it actually goes a long way. The days that I'm rushing or don't feel like doing it, I can tell. You've got 1 body…that's it, just 1, so it would behoove you to find some ways to take care of it before you're in a situation that you can't come back from and end up losing everything that you've worked for.

Being a pro in this industry is about more than just spinning tracks. You gotta be reliable and professional. Show up on time, be prepared, and keep a good attitude. This builds trust and opens up more opportunities.

In the end, vice control is about balancing the fun and chaos of being a DJ with discipline and smart choices. It's what keeps you on top of your game and feeling good, both on and off the stage. Your life can be whatever you want, whenever you want. There's no reason this industry has to swallow you whole like it does so many others. Too many times, we see entertainers succumb to the vices available and go down a dark path of straight destruction, all because they couldn't control themselves. We have to hold ourselves accountable so that we know what should and should not be consumed, and that's not just on a physical level. The company you keep can be detrimental to the decisions that you make and the opportunities that end up on your doorstep. Please take care of yourself and be careful of where you end up in this industry. Set your boundaries, manage your stress, stay professional, and keep your finances in check. That's how you thrive in the fast-paced world of entertainment without letting the vices take you down.

KELLY J:

Self-disciplined people deserve WAY more credit than what's currently being given in my opinion. The world we live in seems to be throwing distractions around at an all-time high: you get a distraction, you get a distraction, everybody gets a distraction! Layer that with social media's influence on people to compare themselves to friends and complete strangers, yeah it's tough. A work in progress myself, a couple of things have helped me so far: my upbringing and F.O.M.O.

My mom was strict my entire childhood and the older I get, the happier I am that she was. Although the pressures to be perfect were self-imposed, my mom introduced and stood on structure: having a routine in place no matter what. So, as a young adult and now an entrepreneur and mom, structure is effortlessly at my foundation. Dead tired, sometimes unsure of solutions, I'd put a routine in place and stick to it until it failed. If it fails, I go in and see what I can change, and then I make a new routine. This is honestly something I didn't see the fruits of until my 30s.

I wore many hats while trying to put together a routine that worked for me as a new mom, and one of those was a club promoter. One of the top promoters in the area mentored me and gave me one of his nights at a popular lounge, along with the actual blueprint. Before social media went out of whack, I'd get up every Monday around 5am. Coffee was an absolute must because I have NEVER been a morning person. After my coffee, I'd go on Facebook and search through the upcoming birthdays. If a woman or popular person in general had a birthday coming up, I'd send them one of the multiple templates I had, inviting them to come to the lounge on my night for their birthday. I'd worked out a deal with the owners, with the help of the promoter, and groups of 5 or more would get a complimentary bottle of champagne.

The birthday people and popular people would also get a personalized flyer, which I also learned how to make with the help of my cousin, who is a professional graphic designer. I'd design their flyer, send it to them, and promote with all of the flyers for the night daily, until the night of. Because

I started promoting and doing these other tasks, I didn't have the time or creative space to DJ as much and would hire my friends and upcoming DJs to open for me. I was paid a base rate no matter what, but if I hit a certain number in sales, I'd get a percentage, and I REALLY wanted that percentage. The base rate allowed me to pay my DJs, so even if I didn't get paid, which happened a lot, they still got paid. I did this every single week for about 3 months until I finally saw a profit, and initially that profit was only $107. All good! Because now I know this routine works. I hit the ground running, which took away from my creativity as a DJ, but opened a new lane of leadership, where I was able to hire my DJ friends, and create new event concepts and opportunities for upcoming and mainstream acts to co-exist at a reputable venue. I was big on presentation, so I invested a lot of money into professional photographers, and videographers, and made sure the venue itself had the best grade of equipment for performers.

Had I not had the self-discipline to follow through with this blueprint, even with it being such a slow start, I would've lost the opportunity to make thousands of dollars in one day. I mean, I was working EVERYDAY but the event itself was once a week. I had leveraged my time, so I was able to do most of my work from home while breastfeeding a very hungry baby Z. I only left her with Sharon for a few hours, one day a week, which gave me the opportunity to handle meetings or DJ other gigs here and there. This grew and grew for about 2 years, until local politics and a drastic shift in social media changed not only the ability for promoters to be seen, but now the ability to reach out to strangers. The growth of both venues in the city and of local promoters duplicating the blueprint to the T, now created a hot mess of an industry. I was putting out fires every other week and my creativity had taken a huge hit. I was over it and went back to my overall goals and saw that this wasn't my fight. Not in this way, not at this time.

The F.O.M.O. works differently for me. Overall, I have a fear of being broke, lol. Working hard and routine comes naturally to me, and I literally get irritated being placed in mediocrity. I have a fear of not being able to retire my mom, of not retiring myself early, and of not being able to get Z the things she needs and some of the things she wants. Of not being able to give back to my community like I want to, of not being able to buy the food that I want to eat. My F.O.M.O. runs deep and actually works as FUEL instead of FEAR. The distractions come, and sometimes a setback or two happens.

But when I think of these things, I snap out of it; It makes me get up and get back to work every time. It would be unrealistic to think that you're not supposed to fall off or get distracted ever. It's going to happen. Sometimes you absolutely need the alone time to realign. With extremely big and unrealistic (to most) goals, that pep talk with yourself is needed first. Your vision is YOURS first, so start with the main character (you) when working on a plan to bounce back. Don't worry about anybody's cup if your cup is empty. And having a cup to begin with helps!

Sometimes, you need your village, be sure to have a good village though. Take your time putting that together, chile. Your village, friends, family, mentors, they can help a LOT. Fall off of your game and go around them. See how long it takes before they tell you to get your sh*t together. Some people enable downfalls, and some people encourage you to get up. My vice control is my vision and my village, honestly. Cause they're quick to tell me when I'm messing up. When they don't, that good ole F.O.M.O. from within is there. It's a balance that I hope anyone looking for it, finds it, for real.

Ang, NAB, and just about everybody that knows me, knows I only drink red wine. It's been that way since I had Z. She's 6 now, and I rarely divert from it… unless I'm doing brunch with Ang, and there it's mimosas, water, or both, lol.

My vices are alcohol and hookah, and I couldn't do either when I was pregnant with Z. After she was born, whether it was not wanting her or my mom to smell like smoke, or knowing I'd have to pump and dump that good ole liquid gold (my breastmilk) if I drank, the discipline to have some control wasn't hard at all. I stopped breastfeeding when she was almost 3, and I was fresh into my 30s. Random sh*t started popping, hurting, food wasn't digesting the same, and I was trying to figure it out! In all of this research, I stuck to what worked, red wine, and hookah, here and there. I simply couldn't afford to be passed out anywhere; everybody knows the DJ who got too drunk to work, and that DJ doesn't get a lot of gigs. And there was always a very short span of time after I finished working before I had to get home to Z; that little girl keeps me in check.

Some people have help with keeping their vices under control. And some need help. I'm not exactly sure that I would have made the switch from hard liquor to completely quitting everything, then going to wine in my 20s if I didn't have Z. She's not the fun police either though. She's truly the biggest blessing I've ever had, and definitely the most entertaining, lol smh. Parenthood might wipe out your desire for vices completely. Or religion. Or past traumas. Who knows. What I do know is that the entertainment industry will bring whatever your vice is right to your face at some point, and you'll be tested on whether or not you have the self-discipline. It happens to everyone, no matter how wealthy or untouchable they may seem. Being the entertainer, even if it's at your demise, is a win for the people looking to be entertained.

Angie T:

Everything is accessible for you, everything except a damn vitamin, electrolyte, or healthcare plan. That stuff you'll have to pay out-of-pocket for, but hey! Let's keep drinking! Now I'm not going to pretend I haven't been there myself. When I first started, I used to drink a glass of wine (or 2 mind ya business) before hosting to calm my nerves. Looking back, I see that it was a lack of confidence on my part. I wasn't getting sloppy or belligerent, but I relied on that drink to ease my nerves and boost my confidence to entertain. My subconscious thought the only way to tap into the life of the party vibe and connect with people was through certain vices.

The F.E.W.:
DJ Kelly J, NotaboiDJ, Angie T

What I've learned is that any vice, when abused, can signal something deeper within you. That's the self-awareness we talked about. It really hit me when family and friends back home would casually mention having a drink, and I would try to correct them, only to realize, "Oh shit, I am drinking every weekend." So, I had to cut that out. Same with food. A lot of these spots serve deep-fried heart attacks, and at 2 a.m., it sounds like a great idea. But the way these back rolls are set up, maybe it wasn't.

Speaking of discipline… let's talk about the gym. When I'm hitting the gym a couple of times a week, I feel amazing. I don't need coffee because I've got the energy, and I can host for hours without getting tired because I'm building my stamina. My clothes fit better, and I can literally see all the benefits. The only thing standing in my way is having the discipline to stick with it and stay consistent.

I'm a cannabis connoisseur, but I recognize that overdoing it isn't good for me and might be a sign I'm avoiding something. Cannabis often gives you that 'f**k it' attitude, where suddenly whatever was stressing me out seems irrelevant. But that can also mean letting people off the hook who need to be held accountable. It gets deep, I know. It's not to say that everyone who smokes is avoiding something. Cannabis has genuine medicinal qualities that have positively impacted many lives. I'm simply pointing out that it's important to do self-check-ins and ask yourself if you're avoiding something by indulging. How do you feel? Annoyed, sad, concerned, or low? I see nothing wrong with having a little dranky drank; it's just the reason behind it that needs to be examined. So, do your self-checks and live your best life.

During my cleanse to move past my grief, I remember that nothing seemed strong enough to take away the pain. I was in ATL, helping with funeral arrangements, and spent an entire day smoking and drinking, yet I still felt numb, still sad, still low, still crying. I wasn't drunk or altered; that's when the lightbulb went off for me. I was scared that my search for something to numb the pain could lead me down a completely different life path. It's like I was watching myself experience this while begging and pleading for help.

When I did a 90-day cleanse, it really opened my eyes to how accessible drinking and smoking was everywhere I went. At networking events, you get a free drink ticket as soon as you walk in. At my own events, the venue would have some for me as well. Customers often offer to buy you another drink and if you say you're just having water, it can feel like you're spitting in their face. It's a balance you have to be okay with, even if it means being labeled the 'party pooper' by others. Discipline is key in every part of life. If you want to get fit and stay in shape, you need physical discipline. For organization and reducing chaos, mental discipline is essential. And if you're aiming to grow closer to God, the universe, or your spiritual source, spiritual discipline is what's required.

My spiritual discipline is an ongoing journey; it isn't something with an end date. I want to be clear: discipline doesn't mean perfection. As TLC wisely advised, let's "stick to the rivers and lakes that you're used to" rather than chasing waterfalls. *snaps fingers poetically*. One thing I learned while trying to get my life back on track is to show myself grace, so I can set a plan and adjust as needed. For example, during my 90-day cleanse, I was committed to no meat. But yes, there were days I succumbed to chicken wings at 2 AM. I had to remind myself not to discredit all the progress I had made. Instead of feeling like I had to start from scratch again, I learned to simply make up for the day and move forward with a fresh start. Starting over always felt defeating, but continuing felt much more achievable. As I write this book, I'm still working on my discipline. I haven't meditated in about three days, but I'm going to be graceful with myself, get down to pray, and pick up where I left off. It's hard when you're trying to balance it all at the same time, so be graceful along your journey. I had the expectation to handle it all at the same time but in reality, I wasn't getting anywhere. I can't speak for everyone, but I know for me, I had to tackle those things one at a time.

Financial discipline came natural for me because I was raised by my grandparents, who were experts at stretching a penny. But as I got older, I realized that even their wisdom had its limitations in today's world. My lil sis Ibi, from Nigeria, showed me a different approach. Even with a higher income, she focused on minimizing her expenses, which at first felt a bit excessive to me. She reminded me of Terry Crews' character from Everybody Hates Chris lol, not as extreme, but close enough. We'd have long talks about building and diversifying a financial portfolio. I then understood why she'd budgeted so hard. Once I adopted her strategy, I realized how practical it really was. This experience reminded me that your circle can impact you in ways you might not expect, regardless of their age. Be open to learning from others. Having more years doesn't mean you have all the answers.

Last but not least, we have to STAY HUMBLE. Getting high off the fame supply can definitely be detrimental. Now, I'm not saying to downplay your success, but letting the praise feed your ego can lead to an 'untouchable' attitude. That's why staying connected to the community is key, because if you stay in the spotlight too long, you'll get blinded by it. There are already enough big egos and wannabes in this industry, so dare to be different, dare to be rare, and most importantly, dare to be you! Ain't nobody like YOU :)

BARS & BEATS

TRACK 8:
Golden Girls Theme Song
Behind The Scenes

NAB:

We started out as co-workers at 88.1 radio station and our friendship evolved over time. Seeing each other was a constant since we worked together so we had no need for really trying to plan dates together. Now, we're all working at separate entities and have to put forth effort when it comes to maintaining our friendship. Now I'll be the first to admit that I work too hard and too much. (They do too) In all actuality, if you don't move your feet then you don't eat when you're an entrepreneur. Starting out, the grind is a must. Then, once you become more seasoned and figure out how to maneuver in this industry, you can scale back. Think about it… when you take a vacation, you're not only missing money but you're also spending money, and that means that the math ain't mathing for me, honey. It's weird because even when taking breaks or trips, I still always find a way to include business in the mix. Being productive, accomplishing goals, and building legacies is my thing. Plus, I actually love what I do, so that makes it even trickier.

Connecting with Angie T and DJ Kelly J is always a double-edged sword because we can try to meet for a bite to eat, but since we do a lot of events together, brainstorming comes out of nowhere. As much as we try, there's always work to be done, so here we go...writing a book, go figure. LMAO.

A few summers back, I told "The F.E.W." that we should go out to an Afrobeat festival in Sac Town provided that we could ALL get the weekend off, which is damn near impossible. Guess what? We did! The cool thing is I have a homie there that wanted to go and said that we could crash at his spot. We were on our way to a 2-day Afrobeat festival, although anytime us entertainers travel for leisure, we're passing up on getting bread. Not to mention we're spending dough as well (cringe), so our thought was at least we could try to meet some of the organizers and possibly collaborate in the future. Let me tell you, there were so many people at this festival that just barely seeing the stage was damn near impossible, so connecting wasn't happening. Oh well, that shit was litty. Each day was exhilarating with all of the food and artists that performed throughout the festival. It started early and ended late, so we were definitely trying to see as much as possible since we barely get days off. Me being a loner, I would often wander off to go be adventurous, which drove them crazy, but I always found my way back. The food was off the chain due to their variety of cuisines, from African, American, Jamaican, Mexican, you name it. We ate as much as we could and of course, I snuck my bottle of booze in…OF COURSE. The sun and the lines were a bit tiring, but we pushed through, being sure to maintain our hydration. Although, one of the days we had to jet our asses up out of there cuz it was a massive crowd of folks that took off running, so the melanin in our skins prompted us to follow. We never found out what happened either. Crazy thing is, they never had the festival again, so I definitely think those shenanigans played a part cuz other than that, the shit was a 10 in my book!

Holidays are typically when we try to make sure we get together at all costs. DJ Kelly J doesn't celebrate but she's always a good sport and goes along with our festivities. Angie T is known for throwing a "Friendsgiving" event yearly, which turns out dope. There's always hella food, liquor, and games. As often as possible, TikToks are on our to-do list, but DJ Kelly J isn't a fan of them, so tons of time is spent on convincing her to do them.

But if they're recorded on Angie T's phone, then that shit is dead cuz we'll beg her for it & sometimes never see it. She'll legit be on our heels about doing a TikTok. I mean she be having us rehearsing and everything only for the final videos that we actually make, never seeing the light of day. I hate that for us. I wonder if that contributes to DJ Kelly J not wanting to do them in the first place. LMAO.

Kelly J:

I'm weak, lmaoooo.

NAB:

Kwanzaa is my day. I chose to stop celebrating Christmas some years ago because I wanted to make holidays more meaningful to my kids and I. We still decorate and go to Christmas festivities, but the gift stuff ain't for us. More often than not, Angie T & DJ Kelly J will come through so that we can get some more quality time in before we go back into overdrive. I try my best to have educational games and lessons that everyone who attends can partake in so they can leave feeling a little wiser and more empowered about their history and the power of the black dollar. Let me not digress.

The F.E.W.:
DJ Kelly J, NotaboiDJ, Angie T

This is Vegas, so we definitely have a drunk story or a "FEW." So, there are plenty of drinking conventions out here, and one day we were able to get together to entertain ourselves. Bruhhhhhhh…why is it so drunk here? The event that we went to was the kind of spot where they rented out a ballroom at a casino, letting you sample UNLIMITED spirits for like 3 hours. How is this even legal? Walking through rows and rows and rows of beer, wine, vodka, tequila, rum, whiskey, gin, & shit I can't even comprehend, was suicidal. Every booth has workers that are literally begging us to taste their drinks, like "come over here"…"no come taste this" swearing that it's the best thing in the world, and they always have a spit bucket for those of us who don't really want their liver to fall out their asshole.

There's usually a DJ spinning, which is when I disappear to find out who they are and how they got booked, wondering why it isn't me, LBVS. Walking past people laid out is the norm, not to mention those that are puking their guts out all so they can keep drinking. We were strolling along and convincing each other to try stuff, having a funky good old time. You see all types of people from different skill levels of drinking, from novices to experts, but they still succumb to the reality of, "How much can you really drink?" If you do the math, within the first row and first 30 minutes you're smashed. Actually, shit faced. I mean, we're laughing, frolicking, taking pics, and meeting other alcoholics, but then it hits you. Usually, I'll be the first to bow out after drinking an unimaginable amount of liquor cuz once the room is spinning, count me the fuck out! In Chicago, we start drinking at a young age, so I've been on bathroom floors praying to porcelain Gods a hundred or so times too many and drinking for fun is kinda old for me. Like how many times do you really wanna be blaming shit on the alcohol? Better yet, who wants to wake up with their millionth hangover? If that's your thing, go off…but I absolutely hate that for you. DJ Kelly J often comes in at a stern second, cuz she be tryna "Wine" herself to death, but we always convince her to drink some real alcohol lol. She is pretty disciplined when we're working or at a meeting, but even Jesus and his disciples get white boy wasted at these events.

Now baby when I tell you that po' Ms. Angie T failed the assignment…hunty. Now she was indulging just like everybody else in the building, but everyone has a limit. That liquor has a way of sneaking up on you, and it affects everyone differently, it's just a matter of time. Let's just say that it was a long, messy, drunk night with the blind leading the blind. Actually, I'll leave the rest of that story for Angie T to tell. If she wants to.

Angie T:

Woah umm excuse me?! See what had happened was I got there late, like 32 minutes before the event was over, so I had to make up for lost time! As soon as I walked through the doors I was on a mission, skipping the small talk with the reps and going straight for the shots. I was tossing those things back like it was juice! About 15 minutes in, I decided to join the rest of the group near the dance floor where everybody in the building was turnt up. I discovered the white chocolate tequila fountain and that damn thing had me in a headlock! I literally couldn't stop eating it. It was soooooooo good, so for the last 15 mins that's all I did. It was a plus that it was right near the dance floor so I'd be doing the cabbage patch right on over to the booth for a refill until they closed.

All was great until it was time to head to the parking lot and it seemed like I may have left my head next to the white chocolate fountain. All I remember is NAB and Kelly J trying their best to get me in the car and then NAB trying to find my apartment I just moved into and waking up on the couch with one shoe on. I remember we had plans

233

to hit up the trap karaoke that was in town after the event but yeah, definitely didn't make that! The next couple weeks were torture for me cause I had alcohol poisoning followed by the flu. It was badddddddddd, but I lived to fight another day and I THOUGHT I put that night behind me *insert side eye*.

NAB:

Dam Ang, you left out some very juicy details but I guess that'll have to suffice! Food is an easy way to get us all together. You can definitely catch us at someplace that has good food, like the Oyster Bar! It's a plus for DJ Kelly J if they have hookah, lol. Another great thing about being in the entertainment industry is that most of our meetings are at restaurants. A lot of us do mutual gigs so we'll find a way to have a business meeting and quality time together. Ya gotta do what ya gotta do, right? DJ Kelly J is the one to remind us that we're friends and to not let business get in the way of that. Angie T is the one that wants a hug when she sees and leaves us...yup that's 2 hugs in a matter of about 3 hours. I'm the one that's like whatever. I just wanna be where the money resides...no cap. Them my girls though!

If all else fails, at least we can show up to each other's gigs in between our own. Supporting one another has pretty much been the foundation of our friendship. As odd as it may sound, we don't really talk on the phone which could potentially solve a lot of our problems with not having enough time to get together. Then again, I'm not a phone person so let me shut my ass up. At the end of the day, we make time when we can and if not, we'll see each other in these Vegas streets.

Kelly J:

I have to mention this one time we went to an alcohol tasting. Picture this: a warehouse with free alcohol EVERYWHERE. Only in Vegas for sure! This was one of the most hilarious meetups with the whole gang from 88.1. There was a woman there that wore a necklace made of pretzels. I asked her where she got it from, but she proudly declared that she made it herself so she always had something on her to absorb the alcohol, PURE GENIUS! Most of us failed the vice control test that day, lmao!

Long story short, I loooooooooove my friends!!! There are very few people that I was friends with before I started DJing that are still friends of mine now. To have that F.E.W., pun intended, is something I never take for granted. Making real friendships afterward seemed so impossible; everybody wants to be a DJ or needs help getting in the industry. It's hard being able to tell who's around because they genuinely rock with you and who is trying to get something out of the deal. For a while I was over making new friends. I tell Ang and NAB all the time, I may not be their best friend, but they're mine! They've been around for some of the biggest moments in my life, good and bad. It's hard to explain our chemistry, but it just is! We know that NAB is going to call every few months to assemble something at her house, and we'll probably always be there if she's cooking. Ang wants to be the cool aunt and kick it with our kids, more than she does with us it feels like. And I'm there to remind them that I'll die if we don't do something together that isn't work related, and it'll help if it doesn't involve bugs or assembling something at NAB's house, lol.

I don't think we'd have each other if we weren't working in the same industry, and if we did meet outside of work, we wouldn't have been as close. Our friendship, along with the framily of coworkers at 88.1 FM, Simply T, Tanisha, Meeka, Miles Low, and later Ambeezy, developed solely because we were around each other around the clock. RIP to our dear friend DJ Certified. From trying to make the station its best version yet, to wanting to be more active in the community, to endless jokes on and about each other, the natural glue that builds in any work environment was also our fate.

The same can be said about my Core DJs family too. There are about 500 of us nationwide, and although building relationships from groups of this size prove to be a true test of memory and effort, and y'all my memory is sh*tty, I'm doing alright. I know my Core family, and make time to know about them all, but I'm only close to a handful of them. Only a few of them live in Las Vegas. I would have never met them casually at a store or event. The support of my Core DJs family has stretched beyond years, allowing me to travel and network far beyond my abilities in Vegas. But the friendship that became family is even more valuable. DJ Shay Money, DJ J Luv, DJ Tiggz, DJ Charlie Hustle, who's the reason why I'm even in the Core, DJ Hollygrove, all the way to the CEO himself, Tony Neal. They are some of the Core DJ family that have become really important in my professional and personal lives. Everybody needs that one person willing to give you a shot, especially in the beginning, and you never know how you're going to react to failure, or a loss, or loneliness, and having the genuine support of people in your industry, people that have seen it all, means everything.

I'll never forget being pregnant with Z and like 4 of my friends were also pregnant. Our babies were weeks and in some cases, days apart. One of my friends who's also in the Core, DJ KimU, one of my friends was here in Vegas, Jess, and the other two were on the East Coast. The mommy group chat got us through some hard times! From trying to wiggle through the emotions, to tips on pain management, and breastfeeding later, that support group of other moms, along with my mom, played an integral role in whatever peace I had during Z's first few months of life.

I get that some people are introverts; they may not exactly want or desire to go out and make friends. It's extremely difficult working in the entertainment industry without them, though. Professionally, friends look out for friends. People that are in positions where they can offer a helping hand and/or hire someone, start with their circle first. Think about how many celebrities, and athletes are related. We see families and affiliates get priority in colleges and jobs all the time. And everywhere else, friends look out for friends. You never know of all the times someone has co-signed for you, or spoken your name in rooms you're not in, to get you in there. No one is completely self-made and thriving.

It's become the norm for many to worry about self-care when things are wrong, but by then it's usually too late. Self-care is just as important when things are going well. That was something NAB and Ang had to teach me, partially because I'm always working and because it was something I never practiced for real.

We started a not-so-consistent-but-we're-working-on-it habit of sound bowl healing days, spa days, and/or massage days together to reset and realign for the many tasks ahead. It DOES make a huge difference, and it's important to remember that you still deserve these things when everything is okay. It allows you to stay focused. It allows the downtime before extremely difficult tasks. It in part, allows you to hear that voice from within saying: you can do this. You got this. The reward then from completing those hard tasks or experiences sits solely in the experience now. Your body seems to be more present, and the energy of it is allowed to help manifest other things, versus working to heal your body.

Angie T:

I love and appreciate these girls because I know they've got my back, even when I'm not in the room. We bring different flavors, and somehow, it just works! I admire Notaboi's fierceness and persistence. She's consistent in doing life however she wants to right or wrong—sometimes it's admirable, and other times she's downright nutz! Lol. Kelly J is the superwoman of the group. She'll be DJing, making flyers, and writing curriculum for her students all at the same time. Loyal as they come and way too friendly if you ask me! Lol. As for me, I think I'm the good balance of both, depending on the situation the wind could blow to the extreme of each side. Sometimes I'm vibing with Kelly J's easy-going ways, and other times I'm ready to set it off with NAB.

Building friendships in this industry has been... interesting. Some people I've met have become my extended family, and I wouldn't trade them for the world. I've been in Vegas for about 8 years now, and the people God has placed in my life are priceless. I refuse to let a few bad apples ruin it, but I'd be lying if I didn't admit that some people I thought were friends or 'framily' even turned out to be predators, lurking for an opportunity. The first time hurt because I let my guard down, trusting them like family, only to realize they were just waiting for a chance to make a move. After it happened a couple more times, I decided I'm better off keeping my circle small and protecting my peace, sometimes it's just safer that way.

BARS & BEATS

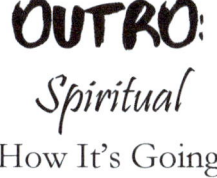

OUTRO:
Spiritual
How It's Going

Kelly J:

I sincerely hope you learned something. About us, about the industry, and about yourself, cause putting this book together was some WORK! We had the main mutual goal to help the next wave maneuver through this mess of an industry with less difficulty than we did. I know for a fact that NAB moved through faster than I did and believe that you can do it faster than she did with the tools and tips we put in this book. Ang is in a slightly different department, but in entertainment nonetheless, literally our partner in event crime, paving the way for hosts/emcees. I hope you see the magic in that. Creating lanes, breaking barriers, having a lot of fun, and establishing financial freedom with your friends is absolutely possible. Plan the life YOU want. Write it down. Look at your goals daily. Surround yourself with people that are assets. Practice discernment like your life depends on it, because it does. Keep liabilities to a minimum, adulthood is already complicated af. Zone out to realign and focus on yourself when you need to. Tap in, building networks and establishing genuine relationships with new people when it's time to. Don't be weird about it, new friends are okay, lol. Have faith and remember that it starts within; pray/meditate AND attach some action to it so that it manifests. Most of all, remember to enjoy the journey along the way.

I was really excited to learn that books are revised and things are added when they need to be. I KNOW we put a lot in here, but we still have a lot more to experience and share. So, I'm telling you to TAP IN with the F.E.W.!

Angie T:

I hope you take some nuggets away from this book. Whatever you dream of doing, just go for it, because if there's anything this journey has taught me, it's that everything happens for a reason.

"Your life can be whatever you want, whenever you want." – **NAB**

Sometimes I can see God's plan clearly, and other times I'm staring off like there's an invisible camera crew filming my life—because seriously, this can't be real. Yet both times, it's worked out in my favor. So, take care of your family, but always put yourself first, listen to your body! Say what you mean & mean what you say and don't let these people play in your face. At least not twice!

NAB:

Alright, we've finally made it to the end! For those of you who made it this far, consider yourself all the wiser. From the beginning of this journey, there was absolutely no way I could have predicted ANY of the wild shit I went through in the entertainment industry. Not to mention, things are still going haywire as I write, so there may very well be a part 2 of this book. The best thing I had going for myself was the fact that I grew up in a musical family who cultivated music in every fiber of my being. Even to this day, our family functions thrive with the essence of soulful melodies playing in the background. My legacy in the industry will continue running through my bloodline, as I have passed on music as a passion to my children and hope that it will bring as much tranquility to them as it has to me. Your story may be different, and you may not have grown up musically inclined, but at the end of the day, if it's in you, then it's for you. You could literally start anything from scratch today! How bad do you want it though?

I started DJing in 2018 and, despite what the naysayers whispered, I retired from corporate America in 2022 to pursue my newfound passion that's been propelling me ever since. Let's not forget, I started with 88.1 radio station in 2019, which has opened up so many doors it's unbelievable, and they just keep opening. Don't second guess yourself, move in silence, and just keep going.

Looking back, I realize how crucial it was to believe in myself and my dreams. It wasn't always easy. There were moments of doubt, times when the uncertainty of it all seemed too much. But every beat, every gig, and every opportunity was a step toward my true calling. Music isn't just a hobby; it's a lifeline, a way to connect with others and express myself.

In the beginning, DJing was just a spark of curiosity, a small idea that grew into a blazing passion. I remember the early days, practicing for hours, learning the ins and outs of the equipment, and experimenting with different sounds. It was exhilarating and terrifying at the same time. But with each mix, I found my rhythm and gained confidence.

The F.E.W.:
DJ Kelly J, NotaboiDJ, Angie T

Following DJ Kelly J around faithfully so that I could absorb her musical expertise was the best decision EVER. She is so mf dope it's captivating. She's not only my mentor but a cherished friend that is near and dear to my whole soul. I will forever be grateful for our relationship and my future plans include retiring her too, cuz her ass works way too damn much, LBVFS.

Leaving the security of a corporate job was one of the scariest decisions I've ever made. The safety net was gone, and I had to rely on my skills, passion, and determination. But that leap of faith paid off. It pushed me out of my comfort zone and forced me to hustle harder than ever. The freedom to pursue my passion full-time was worth every ounce of effort.

Working at 88.1 was another turning point. It wasn't just about playing music; it was about connecting with the listeners, understanding their vibes, and creating unforgettable experiences. The exposure and opportunities that came from the station were beyond anything I could have imagined. It felt like the universe was aligning with my dreams, opening doors I never knew existed. This was where it all began for Angie T and I to nurture a beautiful connection that still stands strong to this day. Her unparalleled gift for hosting has helped me find my voice. As much as I try to stay away from the mic it's dam near impossible so many times I think, "What would Angie say?" That shit is classic, cuz she always knows what to say to rock the crowd and has been motivating me when I'm at a loss for words. It's friendships like this that money can't buy. Get you some!

It can be a lonely road trying to climb your way to the top all while juggling the ins and outs of life. Family life, dating, and maintaining your sanity are things that have to be navigated as well, so get ready! I've yet to master the art of having a successful dating life but fortunately I put my pain of failed relationships into productive endeavors. After every break up, I take on a new project and accomplish more goals. IDK why but working has always helped me heal plus I get to level up. Hence, now I am writing a book. How sway!

My journey in the entertainment industry taught me the power of perseverance and self-belief. It showed me that it's never too late. You might face challenges and setbacks, but those are just part of the process. Each obstacle is a lesson, each failure a stepping stone to success. Hopefully, this book gave you some laughs, gems, and insight into what can help you if you decide that you want to jump into this arena.

So, if you're out there, contemplating a change, dreaming of something bigger, take that first step. Trust in your abilities and ignore the people that more often than not have a lot to say but don't do shit. Be disciplined, work hard, and stay focused. Your passion will guide you, and the doors will open when the time is right. Writing "Bars & Beats" while being "Ladies of The Night" isn't for everyone, but HEY somebody's gotta do it!!!

BARS & BEATS

THE F. E. W.

The F.E.W. (Fire, Earth, Wind) is a visionary collective founded by NotaboiDJ, DJ Kelly J, and Angie T, three pioneering women who draw inspiration from nature's elemental forces—each representing strength, resilience, and unity.

Formed to empower women across traditionally male-dominated industries like music, radio, nightlife, and business, The F.E.W. is more than just a collective; it is a movement designed to amplify female voices and foster meaningful change in these fields.

With deep roots in advocacy, mentorship, and community-building, The F.E.W. strives to create pathways for women to rise, regardless of their stage in life or career. By cultivating a space where women can confidently share their stories and unique experiences, The F.E.W. aims to redefine what it means to succeed in spaces that historically lack female representation.

Through support networks, educational initiatives, and partnerships, this collective empowers women to own their narratives and inspire others.

One of The F.E.W.'s hallmark projects, Bars & Beats – Ladies of The Night, sheds light on the challenges, triumphs, and complexities faced by women in the entertainment industry and business as a whole, blending personal stories with practical wisdom. This book stands as a beacon for women everywhere, encouraging them to navigate their paths boldly, embrace their power, and use their influence to open doors for others.

To join or support this transformative movement, or simply to learn more about the collective's mission and initiatives, visit (http://www.thefewfromvegas.com).

Together, we can build a future where every woman's voice is celebrated and every journey honored.

www.TheFewFromVegas.com

EARTH

DJ KELLY J

DJ Kelly J is a Detroit, MI native that has planted roots in Las Vegas, NV for over 20 years. She's a DJ, DJ workshop instructor at UNLV, author, and an active member in various groups such as the Core DJs, the NAACP, and the Chamber of Cannabis.

As a DJ for over 15 years, she pioneered the advancement of professional minority women in the radio, nightlife, and the corporate DJ industry while consistently serving the community.

@DJKELLYJ

WIND

ANGIE T

Angie T is an award-winning emcee, author, and community leader whose career blends entertainment, advocacy, and impact. Raised in a family of strong women leaders, she carries that legacy forward with a powerful presence on and off the stage. Known for her vibrant energy and unmatched ability to connect with audiences, Angie T has hosted events across the country, leaving a lasting impression everywhere she goes.

Beyond the spotlight, Angie T is the founder of G.L.O.W.™ (Girls Learning Our Worth), a mentorship program that empowers young girls through hygiene education, confidence-building, and life skills. By addressing the often overlooked topic of hygiene alongside self-worth, G.L.O.W.™ helps girls step into their power and shine from the inside out.

With roots as an on-air talent for a Las Vegas morning show, Angie T continues to expand her reach, using her voice to uplift, empower, and inspire at every opportunity. Learn more about her work with aspiring emcees and hosts at angietonair.com

@ANGIET_ONAIR

NOTABOI DJ

NAB: NotaboiDJ is a dynamic force in music, radio, business, and education, celebrated for her vibrant stage presence and influential voice on the airwaves. As the morning show DJ and on-air personality for 88.1 KCEP's "The Wake Up Squad,, in Las Vegas, she energizes listeners daily with her passion and authenticity Mon-Fri 6-10am PST.

Through her company, Notaboi Global Productions, she created Future Frequency Kids™, a hands-on DJ curriculum she designed for elementary school students. The program introduces young learners to music, creativity, and self-expression while helping them build confidence, discipline, and technical skills.

Her vision extends beyond entertainment. She is currently developing a nonprofit dedicated to community healing and holistic health through music, with a focus on empowering underserved communities.

In Bars & Beats: Ladies of the Night, NotaboiDJ shares her journey and insights, offering readers both inspiration and practical guidance to claim their worth and amplify their voices in business and the entertainment industry.

@NOTABOIDJ